THE PRINCESSA

THE PRINCESSA
Machiavelli for Women

H A R R I E T   R U B I N

B L O O M S B U R Y

First published in Great Britain 1997
This paperback edition published 1998
Bloomsbury Publishing Plc, 38 Soho Square, London W1V 5DF

First published in the United States by Doubleday,
a division of Bantam Doubleday Dell Publishing Group, Inc.

A CIP catalogue record for this book
is available from the British Library

ISBN 0 7475 3516 7

2 4 6 8 10 9 7 5 3 1

Printed in Great Britain by Clays Limited, St Ives plc

For Avram

CONTENTS

Contents

THE BOOK OF TACTICS

Contents

THE BOOK OF SUBTLE WEAPONS

EPILOGUE: STRATEGY FOR A WILD PEACE   157

A prince is a man among men, a canny fighter, a steely sovereign who takes what he wants out of life. The term has been one of honor, but the feminine corollary—princess—has been a term of derision, until now.

Katherine Anne Porter said it best: "What a man did only for God, a woman did always for a man." But now a princessa may do for herself. I offer you this parable: Two sisters embarked on a journey. After a long day, they finally arrived at their hotel room. The room was adequate but not comfortable. The younger sister was satisfied, but the older insisted they move immediately. "Each night in my life is as important as any other night," she explained to her weary sister.

A princessa, like Machiavelli's prince, is a woman among women, a canny fighter, a steely sovereign. Take what you want out of life, and remember: Each night is as important as every other night; each day is yours for the taking.

Letter from the Machiavella I Have Become to the Reader, the Princessa of a Troubled, Embattled Domain

❧ I HAVE WRITTEN THIS BOOK FOR you, princessa. Like Machiavelli's prince, you may be sitting alone somewhere safe, wanting to take control of your life, your loves, your problems—the way the young Florentine prince was desperate to take control of a kingdom run amok. At that moment, Machiavelli appeared on the Medici palace scene to tell the prince stories and lessons of how the great Caesars and Spaniards and Popes triumphed over similar woes by fighting.

This book is about war, not the bloody kind, not the kind provoked by Caesar's hatreds or Sun Tzu's deceits or Napoleon's egomania. It's about the wars of intimacy, where the enemy is close enough to hurt you, betray you, oppose you, whether it be a spouse, boss, client, parent, child. It is about war as the route to power. By war, I mean conflict. By conflict, I mean a particular kind of relationship with others, with yourself, and with the world. Conflict is contact. It requires power; it builds power.

In every encounter, one person always has more command over the situation than the other—and may contest you for the things you want. If you lose, you lose your struggle to have a better, fairer, nobler, and sweeter life. Most of us have had no way to express the fight that we keep locked up inside—all those un-reached desires—except through tears of frustration or grief, anger, depression, silence, and submission—all of which can mean instant and irrecoverable losses.

I have found a way for a woman to become the artist of her anger and her desire.

The need for these skills dawned on me one night when I was sitting in the Palace Bar in San Francisco. It was 2 A.M. The piano player had long since fled. But my friends Nora and Judith and I weren't going any-where, even though Nora was on deadline and Judith was trying not to think about where her lover would end up that night—with her or with someone else. I'd promised to call D. when I got back to my hotel, but the sound of his voice was a cold shower I didn't want to feel, the voice of a man who had walked out on me the times I needed him most. What was wrong with us, three women who trotted success around on a leash like a prizewinning dog? Why were we scared of facing our own lives? Why were we warriors nothing, really, but wimps?

Here we were, three formidable women, all capable of negotiating multimillion-dollar deals, but not our own raises. Control freaks though we are, we consistently get involved in relationships where we relinquish control and end up playing the game our lovers' way. Strong though we are, we ask for so little, and then are surprised when we get it. Days when I walk to work in Times Square, I see sign after sign promoting LIVE GIRLS ON STAGE! I may hate what the signs represent but can still appreciate the irony: live girls deserve to be stars; on the street, I pass droves of deadened women, their eyes blank, their expressions passive, their egos reduced by their own negative expectations.

Until now, women have had no language for the fight. We have not been able to express our desire for power. I knew that I wanted power, but I didn't know how to acquire it. When I became a book editor, I found myself working with CEOs to help them craft the books that assured them of an intellectual legacy. I taught myself how to be their publisher, the business-woman they trusted to do well by their deals and their words. When I became their intellectual confidante, I came closer and closer to the center of what made them tick.

One highly reclusive CEO invited me into his inner chamber and asked me to analyze its passageways and corners as if I were analyzing his mind. From their boardrooms to their emotions, I got to study a variety of business leaders and management gurus, trend setters and strategists up close. I became the repository of their confessions, their ambitions, their fears, and so much else. They told me how they made their fortunes. They showed me how to take command of underlings and lieges. Everything I learned from them taught me how to rise in the corporation. How to thrive in a relationship. How to take what I wanted from the world.

Unless we learn to take for ourselves, we are doomed to be princessas-in-hiding forever, not governing a palace but trapped in the Palace Bar, protected by our failure.

You are going to read here about women who have won the rule of their domain. You will learn about strategies to win the wars of intimacy. I will not let you turn away from this quest. The cost of that would be your life, your happiness. "If I'd known how to fight," a friend's mother once said, "I would have lived a better life."

"Learn not to be careful," the photographer Diane Arbus insisted with her students. Careful is safe, peaceful, and on the sidelines of the action.

That night I decided to step into Machiavelli's shoes, to apply all that I had learned finally to my own benefit.

I will teach you war.

✤

EVERYTHING IS BORN in war, Heraclitus said. Babies are born in a struggle. The first tulips of spring bear leaves sharp as knives to fight their way out of the half-frozen earth. There is no shame in fighting.

You will learn in these pages how to conquer an enemy that would kill your dreams. You will see that you can eliminate obstacles to your happiness. You will learn the means by which you can get what you want. Not by assertiveness or aggression. Not by raising your voice, or a fist; not by brutal means but by becoming a presence of great authority. You will learn that winning involves taking for yourself. Most women believe that the way to make life better is to remove bad things from it. Princessas believe in adding good things to it. You will learn the art of implied power, whose expression lies in Strategy. The key to strategy is understanding the power of opposites.

The first law of the princessa is to become a woman who combines opposites.

Aspects of yourself that you think of as contradictory or as opposites are winning partners in war. Weakness comes from believing that you can't be both a lover and a fighter. That is a blunder of the first order. Great warriors understand that *fierce* is the ally of *loving; confrontation* is the ally of *peace; bravery* is the ally of *vulnerability*. Jackie Onassis is always described by those who knew her as a mixture of humility and arrogance, suffering and domination. She gave off a feeling of having been wounded and of being all-

5

powerful. That was the source of her commanding strength.

The strategies of war—or confrontation—depend on changing a fundamental aspect of your self-understanding. A princessa is an artist at making these connections between opposites.

The gods on Olympus are said to have been huge. The reason? They combined opposites. They dominated the battlefields because they had, as it were, a foot in two worlds. The woman who learns to combine opposites becomes a lover-fighter who gets what she wants. She learns to use the skills of one in the domain of the other, and this makes her strong.

I have come to this understanding through two avenues. One is Machiavelli himself. The old courtier, the original Kissinger, admitted that he wrote *The Prince* for men, about men. "Not woman, but man, is the wolf to the man. Not women, but 'men eat one another,' " he wrote. None of his laws apply to women. They apply, by his admission, to cold-blooded users, people with more ambition than conscience. His laws have fueled doctrinaires like Napoleon, Stalin, and, closer to our own time and our civilized wars, the Michaels—Milken and Ovitz—who teach an art of war that is exclusively political.

Machiavelli's prince had to strike a rigid pose: distant, cunning, destructive. He had to be one thing to all people. A princessa has of necessity a different agenda; she needs to disrupt the status quo, rearrange people's perceptions, and thereby gain what is rightfully hers. The princessa came to this earth to rearrange it.

She cannot be a simple, single-minded warrior. She must be the lover and the fighter.

The second avenue of my understanding of war and women comes from a study of the great warrior princessas of history. Tradition (which we know so little of) does not hold us back from true progress. It is the very heart and soul and mechanism of it. Our ancestors were adventurers and discoverers, spies and resisters, pioneers and fighters. Young samurai discovered ways of knowing their bodies' strength through their sensei, or master, who explained how his sensei struck a particular pose, and *his* sensei before that. The princessa, too, can turn to her forebears. To know the history of warrior princessas is to feel a spirit stirring within part of our very nature.

Yet we have had no female *Iliad*. Our knowledge of fighting is too often limited to what a Fortune 500 woman scored in a skirmish. This is a thin view of success—the facts and circumstances of comeuppance and anger, not the strategies and tactics of triumph. It is a view of success based on decades of defeat and compromise. Worse still, it is based on rules of battle that ensure our defeat and our self-resignation.

Women today generally get ahead by relying on male models of power or hardball strategy. They bully, or they blend in; they negotiate, they compromise. Negotiation always results in compromise, something women experience far too often. Such tactics are necessary if your goal is winning. But if your goal is subtler, winning means "besting." Besting demands you compete as much against yourself as against your opponent. It imparts the sense of an Olympic-style triumph: an achievement that leaves losers not defeated so much as breathless, awestruck.

Because they adopt an inauthentic heritage of men's fighting strategies, strong women complain they cannot get ahead. No wonder. They confuse fighting with struggling. They mistake "survival" for "success." *They complain about the glass ceiling, but they have helped erect it.*

With the wrong rules of action, you do not fight for anything, you fight against yourself. For a woman to triumph, she cannot play by the rules of the game. They are not her rules, designed to enhance her strengths. She has to change the game. Play by the rules of another's fight—whoever that may be: man, woman, or child—and you end up strengthening the very rules that favor the opponent. Change the rules and you are playing *your* game, one in which you ignore the simple notions of management and leadership for the strategy of heroism defined by a big agenda, not a step-by-step plan.

By no stretch of the imagination can a woman rely on *The Prince*. Machiavelli's classic work is most famous for being infamous. It advocates murder and treachery; it demeans love. It is the ultimate bible on power of a limited kind. *The Princessa* runs the opposite course. "Princessa" literally means "she who takes first place." The word is an anglicized form of the

Italian *principessa*. Both derive from "principle" and "excellence."

Machiavelli believed a good man hasn't got a chance; he comes to ruin among the many who are not good. The princessa knows that whether people are good or not is irrelevant. She knows she can still get what she wants, not by being an archrealist, as Machiavelli's prince was taught to be, but by different means, and for greater ends than any prince imagined.

She who is governed by principles, not laws, is undeterred. Women always have the power that a commitment to the biggest possible desires—like justice—affords. But they have not used that power.

I have combed nearly a hundred biographies and autobiographies to glean the strategies women have used to amass power. I have concentrated on the rare and breathtaking cases of women who were strategic. I do not mean the women who have amassed wealth or notoriety, per se, women who in our time include Madonna and Sharon Stone. The power wealth provides is not what this book is about. These women have power of a kind. But the power that comes from strategy is greater than the power that comes from money or position.

All in all, there are only a few truly great models to draw from. Most women have approached the turning points of their lives like sleepwalkers. Of the few who were strategists, I recorded their ways, looked for the patterns among them, and finally codified their habits into methods.

The princessa does not traffic in the old business

chestnuts: aggression, negotiation, compromise. She draws on the power that a woman already has inside her but won't express, like a poem that's never quite reached the page, or a portrait stored in her mind's eye. This is a book about how to express that stored-up power, not in a poem or a painting but in everyday life. The princessa knows that the power she holds tightly and doesn't use freely will harm her, weaken her. Like a snake, it can turn around and bite her.

To read this book is to find that *the princessas have all fought one war*. They have fought the war against the intimate enemy by using one strategy: combining love and war into a new whole.

The Princessa is *the lover/fighter, or collaborative antagonist*. She lets fires of any simmering conflict get hot, on the same principle that the heat of the flame turns ordinary steel into a sharp sword. Such tensions and how to create them are the focus of the first half of this book, "The Book of Strategy." Understand the framework of this strategy and you are halfway to winning. The next part of the war game is "The Book of Tactics," and describes the specific points of action that can be used to gain leverage in difficult situations. Superior fighters go beyond both strategy and tactics and learn to use themselves as weapons. Because they pack the force of a bullet, they need not go armed with more than self-knowledge.

Great strategists have been poets, sometimes of the page, sometimes of the public act. Anna Akhmatova, the Russian poet, fought Stalin's repressions with words, not guns or public demonstrations, though historians don't take into account the acts of poets when they unravel the story of how wars are fought. Akhmatova kept alive the spirit and language of poetry. When people had no bread to put into their mouths, she gave them the most bewitching images. She was a sorcerer, whispering her love poems into people's ears (it was forbidden to write them down), knowing that keeping alive the memory of human kindness was the only way for the spirit to triumph when a dictator pitted people against one another, and stole from them any semblance of humanity. In her strategies, a woman fighting a dictatorial boss—or an unreasoning spouse, parent, or child—can find means of recapturing her freedom.

History is full of beautiful surprises. The great social movements of this country were led by women: voter registration, suffrage, abolition, family planning, temperance. Women reached their glory in World War II. More women rose to power in the 1940s than at any other time in history. They became resisters, spies, activists. When the rules are broken, or in shambles, women succeed. When freed from the burden of playing by the rules, they feel they can do anything, challenge anyone. This is vital. *Most women today feel they must play by the rules.* They feel they must be the best damn rule players ever. Yet in doing so they limit themselves. War favors the dangerous woman. Women may love peace and seek stability. But these conditions seldom serve them. Even in corporations, a stable situation is less beneficial to women than a chaotic environment. Princessas understand that opportunities are created in chaos. The trick in times of relative peace is to create chaos and work it.

In the Renaissance, a number of women were able to take charge of empires, among them Elizabeth I, Mary Queen of Scots, and Catherine de' Medici. At the time, boundaries were shifting and old classifications were crumbling. They could not be put back together again by brute force, and subtlety was beyond most kings' understanding. When the empresses and queens failed in their rule, as Catherine eventually did, it was because they fought like men, preferring mastery over risk, negotiation over challenge.

Princessas throughout history have one essential quality in common: *they live their lives as people for whom triumph is a birthright.* They welcome war, conflict, confrontation. This attitude is the second law of princessas, distinguishing them from other women, particularly in the following ways:

1. *From their earliest days, they mark themselves as different from others.*

They are loners. Even within their families, they consider themselves aliens, and they recognize this as power. It doesn't embarrass them; it inspires them. Elizabeth I told herself that if she married, she would be Queen of England. But alone, she was both King and Queen. Married or not, princessas stand apart.

Contemporary psychology praises the value of women's "connection" and relationships. But *the powerful women of history coveted the power of separateness.* It gave them the opportunity for more than self-confidence: "self-love," which poet Walt Whitman described in his phrase "I inhabit my soul," was a feeling they understood. Like children and great wild cats, Freud said, powerful women seem self-contained, mysterious, and this accounts for the fascination they exert on others.

Are such women born extraordinary? Or do they become extraordinary because they set themselves apart, in a psychological atmosphere where they are measured against no one's standards but their own?

Joan of Arc never tried to play down the differences that set her apart. She believed in them until they took on a reality of their own. From her early adolescence, she talked of freeing France from English rule. People thought it strange that a young peasant girl who couldn't read or write had such ambitions; but the more she spoke of them, the more she and others acted as if they were true. This, you will see, was not just a defining mark; it was a key element in her strategy and in the strategies of all the princessas.

2. *They never consider themselves brave.*

Princessas feel they are doing no more than what can be done. They may know they are smart, even unique. But they don't call themselves brave. Dian

Fossey, the primatologist, said heights had always made her scream "like a baptized baby." But once she got into the jungles of Africa, she climbed ravines with the gorillas of the mist she avidly studied. *These warriors relax in the face of danger the way other women relax in front of their TVs.* In a tough situation, they behave as if they have already won, because they don't believe they can lose. They go into battle with a winner's calm. The poet Rainer Maria Rilke said, "Follow your fear." That is what heroic women do. Their greatest power comes in ridding themselves of the very thing that shamed them (like Dian's fear of heights) and making this old fear their source of pride.

3. *They treat destiny as their mentor.*

From the time she was a Milwaukee schoolteacher, Golda Meir felt herself called to achieve something great. Even when she was grading papers, or later, scratching crops out of one of the poorest desert kibbutzim in Israel, her second voice—destiny—was her mentor. She never listened to the voice of complaint or exhaustion, or to any advisors, as closely as she listened to this second voice.

Know your voice, women are told. But princessas have always listened more deeply—to the second voice in all of us. They say this voice speaks from a standing position, from destiny. The word "destiny" has a history as a sailor's term, meaning to align your ship with nothing earthbound, to point yourself in the direction of the stars. When she was three years old, Juana Inés de la Cruz refused to eat cheese because she had been told that it made one slow-witted. She didn't know why, but she knew she'd need her brilliance for some role fate was preparing. In a few years, this seventeenth-century child would grow up to become Sor Juana, one of the great lyric poets, saints, and iconoclasts.

There is a moment in freed slave Sojourner Truth's diary when she says freedom became too hard; she didn't want to have to earn her own keep anymore or make her own decisions. She decided to sell herself back into slavery to be taken care of. On her walk back to her former master, the second voice stopped her. "I have two hearts inside me," Sojourner said. Princessas also need two hearts; otherwise, the voice of self-defeat becomes too strong.

4. *They revel in their emotional lives.*

Women have been made to feel small or silly when expressing their emotions. "Emotional" has come to mean the opposite of "rational." Controlling one's emotions is regarded as the height of supreme power. But princessas aren't fooled by such notions. They are extreme in expressing joy, pleasure, concern. *Pushed to a boiling point, they don't get outraged; they get outrageous.*

Desire is the key; it reframes reality. Desire makes Lady Macbeth the most powerful woman of Scotland.

Everyone in Shakespeare's play follows her agenda before their own. She pulls the future to her—she creates the future—because she, alone in the play, demonstrates the greatest desire. A princessa I know tells this story: "One night my ten-year-old son wanted to find a duck restaurant we had been to a year before in Santa Fe. No one could remember where it was, so three adults and one child set out in search of it. Hours later, we still couldn't find it. We were hungry, but ready to keep plowing ahead, when my friend grabbed my son by the shoulders and said to him, *'Do you see how desire rules the world?'* No one else much cared where we ate, but here we were, following this child around because he alone had the desire."

Princessas express their desire with a diva's virtuosity. They don't hold back. They don't doubt their desire; they feel entitled to their wishes, and they use the potency of them. Isadora Duncan got her first break into stardom by calling on one of France's great impresarios, not just asking for a job but asking for the leading role. She claimed she was "the spiritual daughter of Walt Whitman," whose essence she promised to reincarnate on the stage. Her claim was outrageous. Her desire won her the lead part, though she had been too poor growing up to have had a dance lesson, much less to have danced onstage. It's said that a woman is like a tea bag; it's only when she's in hot water that you realize how strong she is. In hot water, women's desires boil.

5. *They don't believe that life requires you to choose between love and power.*

Power is a kind of love, and love is a kind of power. One kind of love, the most familiar kind, draws two people together in a cocoon of two-against-the-world. But the other, rarer kind of love is political or public love. This love creates a solidarity between a person and everything in her life. A woman who recognizes public love regards nothing and no one as firmly opposed to her. Every enemy is thus a potential ally. She gets close to her enemy much as she would to a beloved. She is keen to strengthen the enemy, not weaken him or her. She uses truth as a weapon when every Sun Tzu or Stonewall Jackson advises one to "mystify, mislead, and disguise."

With all these strengths, why aren't whole kingdoms run by princessas? So many princessas have won partial victories at best. They win battles, they lose wars. What I have seen of women and power, not just today but in history too, has grieved me. *Underlying our partial successes is a distrust of our own strength.* Our secondary status has left us with a legacy of self-doubt and, in the most extreme cases, self-loathing.

Women *are* the fiercer sex. The Greek poets and philosophers trembled before women. Nearly every god of war they named a goddess: Nemesis (revenge), Artemis (sacrifice), Athena (battle), the Furies (anger). It's a Greek parade of women armed with the

17

kiss of death. Nor was this pure nightmare-fantasy. From Custer to Vietnam, soldiers tell tales of how it was the native women, not the men, who would destroy the corpses of the enemy out of hatred. There are Hitlers, there are Napoleons; but there are no male Medeas who would sacrifice their own children for their aims. We are not talking murder here, when we talk of princessas. We are talking about power, strength, and ultimate sacrifice.

Then why so many defeats? One reason is that women fighters are most often motivated by revenge. Revenge means righting a wrong, saving a reputation, defending the dead. Energy is much better spent fighting *for* something tangible for yourself, like the freedom to do important work. To fight for yourself and your aims is not selfish. Women are not hoarders. The principle at work in princessas is that when they have more, they give more, liberated from a mindset of scarcity that is always whispering, "Will I have enough time, enough strength, enough to give?"

Benazir Bhutto, Pakistan's former President, had a long apprenticeship to power, studying with the men who comprised the leadership of Pakistan: her father, brothers, uncles, and cousins. She waited until massacre and fate left no one else but her to assume the presidency of her country. She took on the post in order to avenge her father's assassination, and "to fulfill his wishes," she says. When she visited his mud-covered grave, sprinkled with a few flowers but otherwise unmarked, she would have cried, she says, but she refused to give in to "womanly tears." She bowed to kiss her father's feet, but in that unmarked grave she couldn't be sure how he lay. And then she set out, making her enemies pay, *building nothing worth building* in her vengeance, settling scores, teaching enemies a lesson, acting as policeman of her country—following, in other words, the methods of Machiavelli's prince. As you will see, such behavior always results in a win that is either temporary (at worst) or less than you deserve (at best). As a fighter, Bhutto is a sister or daughter with a grudge, with undoing as her motive. All revenge will get her is a temporary rush of satisfaction, but nothing to hold on to or take pride in. Remember Antigone, who was condemned by the king after she gave her brother a decent human burial? Antigone won the battle: Creon eventually repented, but at the cost of his son's life as well as her own. Antigone was brave as they come, but not strategic. *She lost for the sake of winning.*

Another reason women often lose is that princessas follow the strategy of love and war in their professional lives but diverge from it in their personal affairs. *Time* magazine called Rebecca West "the world's No. 1 woman writer" in 1947. In her work, she fought like a princessa. Love of language, of form, of audience, of her gifts, guided her strategy and actions. But in her personal life, vindictiveness and overinvolvement characterized her strategies. She kept reacting, expressing her anger, limiting the battlefield. Her lovers, her son, all grew cold toward her and kept their distance. At the time of her death, the only people close to her were a few professional friends and acquaintances.

Anger and hurt never win a war. Nelson Mandela found that black and white South Africans who had lived in constant fear of each other had become so accustomed to having less that they no longer thought they could achieve much of anything. He addressed their fears in his 1994 inaugural speech, calling for those qualities of strength and power he knew to be present beneath that fear:

Our deepest fear is not that we are inadequate. Our deepest fear is that we are powerful beyond measure. It is our light, not our darkness, that most frightens us.

We ask ourselves, "Who am I to be brilliant, gorgeous, talented, and fabulous?" Actually, who are you not to be? . . . Your playing small does not serve the world. There's nothing enlightened about shrinking so that other people won't feel insecure around you.

And as we let our own light shine, we unconsciously give other people permission to do the same.

And in Mandela's words we find the third law of the princessa:

*As we are liberated from our fear, our presence automatically liberates others.**

* My italics.

You will learn here why women have feared conflict or suffered from something I call power anorexia. You will learn to manage the crippling tension in situations in a brand-new way. You will learn to fight strategically. You will learn to "best." You will learn to win the wars on your own terms.

Mahatma Gandhi altered hundreds of years of British rule in India with his strategy. He asked his friends to call him "Mother" in recognition of how he loved to fight like a woman: brave cowardice—Satyagraha— he called this style of fighting, which he distinguished from the "manly" fight that left some people brutalized and turned others into enemies for life. Martin Luther King, Jr., used this style of fighting to change the state of race relations in this country. Even boxer Sonny Liston loved to dance in the ring "like dust in a mote of light," according to writer James Baldwin. When an opponent threw a punch, it never landed on him. His strategy, pure princessa, was to fight *his* game and let others swing away at the empty air.

Along the way, you will train your eye to appreciate something new: action. Your look, your talk, your inspiration, will be reassessed from the perspective of how strategic—or action-oriented—they are. Most women react. They work to "exceed performance expectations." They "outperform" men. If men work ten hours, they work twelve. Reaction isn't effective action. No wonder we still don't have the top jobs, or the love we want. No wonder novelist Tom Robbins joked, "Women live longer than men because they're not really living."

These laws and strategies will enable you to shape the events of your life according to your design. Such books have been written before about sex and relationships—from the *Kama Sutra* to Helen Gurley Brown. But none has been written like this about power.

Men and women will find themselves asking in the near future: Why fight like Machiavelli when we can fight like Machiavella?

It's time you governed your life the way princes have governed their kingdoms.

—Your author, in her nom de guerre
of Machiavella

THE BOOK OF *Strategy*

⚜

The art of the princessa is to balance the
terror of being a woman with the wonder
of being a woman.

I

A Princessa Discovers Her True Strength by Knowing Her Enemy

WOMEN HAVE ALWAYS BEEN SPIES. We've spied on our fathers, brothers, husbands, and bosses. We've seen power and its perversions. We, too, seek power, but not for its own sake. We are on a mission: to get our desires, our aims, accomplished. It is our mission that drives us in the face of others' disapproval, and in opposition to our serving their needs. This might be a raise we're worthy of, a chance to do great work, to live in a welcoming home and world instead of a place where we are ignored or, worse, mistreated. To become the princessa you are meant to be will require awakening the spy deep down.

The spy is the ultimate outsider eavesdropping on the strategies of princes, kings, generals, governors, husbands, and sons. The task is to infiltrate, gather information, and then use it. Women often stop short of using the information they gather as spies in the house of power and love.

The first strategic strength to acquire is the power of seeing, hearing, and knowing your enemy. The second strength is in using what you know.

A spy sees into the heart of people and gathers a dossier of intelligence on what makes them tick. Her behavior causes others to react to her, and in ways that serve her agenda. For instance, a spy can ease a confession out of a source. A spy can change the course of nations and people not by bloodshed or hurt but by using her implied, barely demonstrated power. She is subtle, canny, and active.

A spy is who she says she is, but her hidden agenda has the force to convert the enemy. Spies change the game rather than play by the rules. An antagonist, opponent, straggler, or naysayer may not even know he's been conquered and won over to her agenda.

As spies, women know more than they realize. How, then, do they find a way to use that knowledge? How does a spy convert her knowledge into power? First, she transforms it into a conflict, forcing the enemy to react to her on her own terms. She directs the game.

A spy at war sees, and uses what she sees. We know how a new life emerges out of a bud or a womb. But we haven't observed with the same microscopic vision how a relationship that develops out of a seemingly amicable, generous encounter can turn harsh or even destructive. Consider this episode, caught in slow motion to reveal its subliminal meanings:

A client betrays a spy and takes her to a lavish dinner to apologize. He is a brilliant man whose partnership she coveted and worked hard to get. But he has chosen her competitor, who took a backseat and then, in the final hour, topped her bid for the job. How is she to maneuver in the face of the tough ego blow handed to her?

She could cut this Judas out of her life, in an effort to punish his betrayal. But vengeance, remember, is ineffective. So is any tit-for-tat response, though weak warriors love this measure and rely on it because of its promise of instant gratification. But not a warrior-princessa. She knows this man has many things she wants, and that she is in a position to trade them or take them. These include contacts and insider information as well as the excitement of his presence. Why should she cut him out of her life to make a point she will remember but he won't?

"I'm sorry," he says to her as they sit down. He orders a nonalcoholic drink, a Shirley Temple. He mentioned once that he had been an alcoholic. Now he is reformed—a man of severe passions, kept in check. Drink is only one of them. *One is a giveaway for all. Every act contains an enemy's entire strategy*. A princessa watches her enemy. Often it is in his smallest, most innocent gestures that he gives himself away. An enemy, an opponent, always gives himself away, no matter who he is, no matter how clever he is at disguise.

How does the spy react when she sees a clue? She understands it for what it is: his weapon of self-defense against her. Then she disarms him of his own weapon and uses it against him. There is no more effective weapon to use against an enemy than the one the enemy himself is using. "Use the master's tools to destroy the master's house," Aesop's small, clever animals are always advised in their war against big predators. The spy who locates this weapon is on her way to winning.

So she watches. She considers the possibility that this drink contains the truth of this man. The princessa knows that most people deny themselves the things they really want. By figuring out what the enemy secretly wants, she knows how to change the war to get what they both want. Just as this man won't touch a real drink, he denies himself strong friends, partners, collaborators. What if he has flirted with her offer, her willingness to help him develop his work, precisely to say no to her because what she represents is like everything he craves? If so, he betrays himself, not her.

A spy knows this rule of thumb: People do to others exactly what they do to themselves. This man will deny her requests, much as he has denied himself his own desires. A spy also knows that no matter what a person talks about—his sports team or a salad—he's really talking about himself, about hopes or fears he cannot directly utter—his top secret agenda. She uses all this information to build a "shorthand" profile of the person facing her—not as he would like others to see him but as he truly is. She doesn't need to know his biography to reach this understanding. A few clues suffice. This man wants less out of her than the situation might lead her to suspect, which she will soon find confirmed. He doesn't know what she wants of him. And he hasn't grasped, as she has, that both of them can engage in another kind of fight, a joined fight, and win a bigger war than is possible to win in this single encounter. *Every enemy, the spy knows, is a future ally for a war that is bigger than he can see.* That difference in perspective gives her leverage.

So when he boasts about his brilliance and how his clients are amazed by his intellect, she doesn't grimace. She doesn't fake enthusiasm. Every assertion of his ego is something she neither affirms nor denies. Instead, she will neutralize his boasting. *Her first order of business: she must change the battlefield.* Let him know that this isn't a contest to prove which of them is stronger or who has hurt whom. She will challenge him her own way. *First, neutralize an opponent's bid for control. Then take power.*

He is trying to win on his terms by getting her to surrender. Boasting done, he switches to a gambit where he attempts to minimize her contribution to the project. In fact, the very idea for the project was hers. Adding insult to injury, he tells her his decision wasn't based on money, though the competitor's bid nearly doubled her own. He tells her that "the price of love is fifty thousand dollars," meaning he would have signed her contract if the difference between the offers had been that. His feelings for her went that far. She knows that her plans for his work would reap greater profits as well as acclaim. But he maintains that his decision was fair and perhaps even in her best interest.

Enemies often try to persuade you that they act fairly, honestly, even for your own good: the boss who insists you pull out of a venture because some behavior on the client's side is annoying may—in truth—not want you to reap the glory of the deal. Or a lover will refuse a request in order to teach you to appreciate all the things he has already done for you (as if someone's keeping a balance sheet in which your additions column doesn't count). Or a client, broker, doctor, will lecture you generously with their knowledge but stop short of generously listening to you.

Intimate enemies often sound generous. In reality, they try to sideline a princessa by convincing her she is the problem, her desires are at fault. "I got you out of this difficult deal," the boss might say, expecting your thanks, though you know that your difficult deal would have been a windfall for your career. "I remembered your birthday," a husband might say as an apology for forgetting your anniversary. But the question with this man at the table remains: If the money didn't matter to him, why didn't he make amends, like immediately send her fifty thousand dollars' worth of new business? He isn't sensitive and he isn't generous, and this isn't dinner. It's war.

Know yourself, know the enemy. The princessa's task is to pry open the lock on who the enemy is, and what his secret strategy is. Of all the weapons she can use to unlock his strategy, one of the keenest is the "Five Whys." When an enemy says X, ask why. Whatever answer he gives, ask why again, ask (yourself or him) why that particular answer, then ask another why of that answer, and another. At the fifth why, you have information you can use in creating your own strategy. When you trace another's behavior back to its cause, you get to the heart of the antagonist's strategy. The Five Whys let you *see beyond what he wants you to see*. See beyond his strategy and you won't be forced into reacting to his actions. You will act in a way that makes him respond to you. That makes the battle yours to win.

First the spy asks, "Why did you give your business to someone else?" Notice she does not ask, "Why did you betray me?" A spy avoids blame because that will send her spinning into circles of self-doubt and confusion. Her first why is purely factual: Here's the situation; why did it happen? The answer according to this man: to get a better deal.

The second why: Why did it seem to him like "a better deal"? Answer: Because her competitor promised him that he'd already done enough work. Performance standards were not so important, which pushed her competitor to the forefront. The third why: Why weren't standards important, given that he values his brilliance? Answer: He wants to assert his strength, not test it. She has misunderstood the source of his pride, thinking it depends on his accomplishments. His winning strategy for most things is saying one version or other of "yes" that really means "no." No booze, no strong women, no "proof" of any kind. The spy has followed the wrong strategy until now, pushing him to produce more and better work. But his win comes in backing away. Early on, she wasn't watching or listening strategically.

So the fourth why has to deal with her. Why did she go her usual work-till-dawn distance to impress him? Because she doesn't trust her ability to win unless she gets overly involved in a situation, forcing it to a favorable conclusion, doing everything she can to make it come out brilliantly. *But is that the only reason? The spy must keep asking herself this.*

Fifth: Why does she get overly involved? Because that's what she thinks real power is. She's seen in men that power means control. The more involved she can be in a project, the better her ability to control its outcome. But that is a vestige of her old ways; she knows more about power's secrets than that. She has made a strategic error, putting her faith in control; now she must compensate for it.

The next scene unfolds like a B movie, because *when people don't believe in what they do or say, their actions become intensely stagey.* "I get the feeling you're brittle," he tells her, "that you've been hurt by men, and that you break." He snaps the breadstick in two. This man's transparent observation is designed to appeal to the woman's sense of weakness, her desire to be taken care of, but his breadstick soliloquy hasn't described her at all but, rather, the person he would like to convince her she is. He says, "And to complicate things further, we're attracted to one another."

With his claim to understand her, he is trying to make her distrust her own knowledge of herself, and convince her to see herself through his eyes. It's his coup de grâce. Most women hear the music of this— the caring tone—but they block out the words' true meaning, which the Five Whys invariably reveal.

Whether through seduction or rejection, women have been made to feel small, the prey in men's war games. Women often conspire in their own destruction.

True desire is bliss. But that's not what this scenario is about. This man says he's attracted to her, but is he? Or does he need to score a point, not a hit? She doesn't want to react to his bold statement when the truth of his strategy lies somewhere else. Even if he does desire her, or the work she could have helped him accomplish, he won't ever give himself a full swing at triumph, just as he won't drink anything stronger than a Shirley Temple. His desire for her is not what this is about.

The spy has taken all this in. Now she becomes the princessa. She reels him into her kingdom.

Knowing that *the truth is a powerful weapon because*

people are too weak to resist it, she tells him she understands what is going on here. She says, "I'm not brittle. That's not me at all. Just the opposite. You're guarding yourself against a lot of strong influences. You flirt but you don't drink. You don't want me in the way you've just said. But I love working with you, and you I bet want something else I can give you." Good, she thinks, he is paying attention; she's jolted him out of his belief that he can or should seduce her, or that his power is greater than hers.

"If you'd chosen to do business with me, I would have gotten great work out of you," she says. "I would have gotten things out of you that you didn't even know you had. That's who I am." Now, with any luck, he feels *he* has been betrayed, by his own decision. She has used his weapon—his betrayal of her—against him. Now he is challenging his own reading of reality.

She continues: "You think you've hurt me. But you haven't even betrayed me. There is still a lot of good work we can do together, free of the pressure of your other project. We like and respect each other. Let's figure out what we can do to the rest of the world." *When a princessa changes the tone of her voice and demeanor from challenging and confrontational to tender, she does it abruptly.* She knows that to take charge of the tone of a meeting is crucial.

Notice she doesn't fight the wrong battle—his stated goal of bedding her. Instead, *she recognizes his bid for power and neutralizes it.* She neutralizes even his apology, whose undertone is: *I've hurt you; I'm that strong*. The clear message of her response is: *You can't hurt me; I don't break; I'm stronger than you could ever know. And you are stronger than you know. You don't need to be seduced by others, and you don't need to seduce me in turn to prove anything.*

By showing him she understands the power spinning across this table, she is on her way to winning an ally and a war.

How does she get what she ultimately wants? She saves that for another time. A spy isn't in a hurry. She trusts that the future will provide. She trusts that she will prevail in getting what she wants. Thus she is spared from reacting. React to another's fight and you get caught up in your enemy's war, not your own, which means you do not play from a position of strength. To rush a win would be to scare him; and it's clear that this man is already frightened of many things—especially good things. She doesn't need to walk away with a clear victory now. Each advance like this builds her strength, increases her resilience for the next campaign.

The chapters that follow will break down this process step by step so that you can trace how the princessa reaches the point where she can expect and receive so much from others. For now, it is important to see that she has asserted herself not in anger, not in sympathy, but in a shared power for both of them. By leveling his power as she has done, he cannot act against her interests with his trusty weapons. He is left defenseless and looking to her for the next step. She has changed the game on him.

The cleverest part is that she has used much more than her own keen intelligence and strength. She has used his intelligence and strength as well. Both are on their way to fighting *her* war.

II

What It Means to Be Feminine and the Art of Micropower

A PRINCESSA MUST ACT — *STRATE-gically.* By refusing to act strategically, she is literally an "idiot"—from the Greek for "private person"—someone who refuses to acknowledge that life is war and one is meant to fight. Female idiocy is the counterpart of male lunacy. And it is just as dangerous to society. "Men see the world as by moonlight which shows outlines of every object, but not the details," novelist and critic Rebecca West wrote. Women see into the details, which is indicative of their nature, but they get swallowed up by them and don't act. A princessa must see and act.

Power used to mean control over many people, enormous holdings, empires, nations, corporations.

The wider your span of control, the greater your power. Today the only power worth having is micropower, the power to act in small, tight, dangerous spaces. Strategy is the art of maneuvering by using nothing more than a gesture or by acting on the merest perception. Armies are often a detriment; full-scale battle plans, a nuisance. A princessa realizes that her life is dependent on how her own moves orchestrate others' moves. Strategy is her cure against idiocy.

Learn the art of this war and as a woman you will balance the terror of your sex with the wonder of it. The terror lies in constantly being seen as a threat and diminished because of it. The wonder is that the more womanly a fighter becomes, the more she wins. Women love the danger that calls for the small, evasive actions that have major impact. The spy delights in pulling off an "impossible" win. Gertrude Bell, advisor to Arab kings, toyed with the rules. She smuggled guns and maps into the desert. She wrapped her rifle in a lacy white petticoat (which she called "aggressively feminine"). At one point, the chief customs officer saw some maps covering one end of her gun case. She saw that he saw. And then she did the outrageous. She engaged him, her enemy, as a coconspirator. She kept on talking to him about the calmest, most mundane subject: the weather. The contrast of guns in lingerie, of chitchat in the face of real danger (men were shot by the Arab guards for less)—such "small" tactics often disarm gatekeepers who guard the freedom or rewards you want. If they know they

can't keep you out/down/sidelined, they often don't
bother to try.

What "womanly" means in this strange, seemingly
contradictory context of fight is the princessa's exper-
tise.

III

How to Be Brilliantly Disruptive

In the princessa's situation, normal rules do not
apply. Obeying the law becomes a dangerous
addiction. Flaunting it is the way to succeed.

EVERY WORD IN THIS BOOK WILL
lead you to that overall strategy.

The great generals had an easier time with relationships: they could wipe the enemy off the face of the
earth. You cannot do this. In intimate wars, the person who wields unfair advantage over you may be
your mother, your boss, your spouse or lover, your
child, the ghost of your own desires long denied. Anyone or anything with a hold on your emotions has got
you by the short hairs. You must love them and fight
them, both at the same time. Obeying the rules is
obeying their rules—and the worst thing you can
do. Rules are the fiction of whoever takes the lead.
But the rules result in predictable wins. Rewards

are greater when you create change by flaunting the rules.

That is why the warrior/princessas described here will seem at first a strange lot. There is something extreme about them. They defy easy categories. History remembers most of them not as spies or even fighters but as anthropologists, saints, singers, poets. After all, the real work of poets, dancers, performers *is* spying— yet each of them works in full view of an audience. A poet like Anna Akhmatova will write of love and at the same time secretly intend for her words to change a person's outlook and thereby free her. Poetry such as Akhmatova's becomes like a spymaster's code, unlocking others' secrets to influence them to bold behavior or loosening the grip of an unwanted antagonism.

Joan of Arc was a brilliant military strategist. But she was also a simple peasant girl of whom nobody expected anything much. It seems inconsistent to have been both; but in this double nature lay her power. Was Akhmatova a poet of love or a fighter whose words challenged Stalinist terrors? The answer is: both. Was Billie Holiday a brilliant singer or a warrior who brought the message of black suffering and her own desires to anyone who would listen? Both. A spy doesn't fit simple categories; she creates them.

When put to the test, women act as spies. In the French Revolution, "blood sisters" learned to manipulate a political system that excluded them. They wrote under their husbands' names, they dressed as beggars to carry secret messages, they disguised themselves as men and bore arms for their cause.

The brilliance of these women consisted in their being half spy, half flaunter. Like Persephone, who lives half of her year in darkness in the underworld—a punishment for her defiance of a god—and the rest in daylight and glorious bursting spring, every woman has gone underground. Upon surfacing, she brings with her the memory of where she has come from, so that "with all her bright beauty there is something strange and awesome about her," because she had seen something few have seen, in the darkness.

Persephone, like the spy, like the great princessas, operates in two worlds. Joan of Arc was a master at mixing the categories of the hidden and the obvious, the serious and the ultralight. On her first march into enemy territory, Joan came face to face with a young English lieutenant whom she was to fight the next day. It was late and dark and the lieutenant mistook her for a boy out on a joyride with her buddy (who was as young as she was and her sergeant). He asked if the stranger had seen the "Maid of Orleans," as she was called. Joan said yes, she had seen her. "Tell me about her," the lieutenant asked. Joan told him everything about herself, including her plan for setting fire to the bridge the next day, once she and her troops safely crossed it and trapped the enemy on the other side. Her own sergeant could not believe his ears. She had given away their strategy to the opponent. The English lieutenant rose to his feet. "Then I will burn the bridge myself," he declared, "and force the Maid into a contest with me. Her troops are no match for mine." "If you like," said the half-hidden Joan, "I can burn the bridge for you tonight." The lieutenant accepted. He would give his troops a good night's rest before they moved in confidently on Joan. She headed back to her camp to gather her men, then rode past the sleeping enemy, crossed the bridge, burned it, entrapping her enemy—as she had promised—in his camp, and in his stupidity.

What has Joan's example to do with a princessa fighting her own wars? Everything. She told the truth, she fought a war by her own rules, not her enemy's; and found he would play by her rules—without knowing what was happening. She flaunted all the rules by which authority lived and died. This is the work of a great spy and a true princessa.

The method of her change-the-game style of battle is called confrontational cooperation. To a warrior who is also a lover, who combines ferocity with gentleness, the strategy of confrontational cooperation comes naturally. Think of the fire that for all the violence of its heat sharpens the sword. When you find yourself in a tough situation, toughen it a bit more. Let the conflict rise. Nurturing women are loved and cherished. But women who achieve the heroic do not do this simply by wearing a well-pressed Armani or moving to a good address or scoring a high grade point average or wearing the finest underwear in case they are hit by a bus. *The degree to which a princessa is cooperative must always be balanced by the degree to which she is disruptive.*

✦

TO BE BRILLIANTLY disruptive, make your own rules the rules of the game.

Playing by your own rules is critical because life and war and all their many games are not set up for you to win. No one wants you to succeed. Least of all you. A woman destroys her triumph out of guilt over winning. Other women, and men too, would prefer to see you defeated. Even if you did succeed in spite of these negative distractions and ill-feelings, you'd end up winning on terms other than your own. A princessa requires happiness, satisfaction, true love, money, and freedom. Men tend to be happy with less.

Don't practice this strategy if all you want is help in getting your assistant to type your letters. Or if you want to win back a straying lover. Or if you crave acknowledgment from a self-centered boss. The lessons in this book are meant for bigger prizes. They are strategies for getting the things you really want—the more the better. Opportunity, not mere praise. Love and trust, not obedience. Surprise, not predictibility.

A friend who is an economist told me of a meeting she had with a great teacher of philosophy and religion. She had tried for years to get him to answer her letters and her entreaties to study with him. Every so often he took a few students whom he taught his unique principles about living wisely. She knew he worked these people brutally hard to dismantle their narrow notions about themselves and the world. Many could not withstand the rigors or even the discoveries. Others said the experience gave them a new lease on life. To her surprise, she heard he was giving a lecture, something he rarely did, in her area. She went to the lecture, and afterward introduced herself. He said, "A few friends and I are having dinner tonight. Join us."

She was excited beyond belief and arrived at the restaurant well before the appointed hour. She waited patiently, even as it got very late. Then fear and disappointment hit as the other diners left and it appeared as though the restaurant would shut down for the night. Suddenly, a taxi pulled up. Out stepped the philosopher and several students. They greeted her warmly; one of the students seated my friend next to their teacher—a place of honor.

It didn't take her long to ask again if she might study with him. "Perhaps," he said. "You know that if you accept the challenge, the work will be difficult. In the course of it, however, you will notice certain changes. You will probably gain ten or more years on your life. You will be happier than before. Your husband will find you more compelling. Your children will see in you a woman to admire. Your own students will praise you. Your work will be widely read and seriously discussed." My friend was elated. What could be better! Yes, she was about to reply, I'm ready, I'm yours, when the teacher turned to her again and said, "If that's *all* you want."

She, an economist, a woman of careful means and measures, was faced with the puzzlement of the simplest word of her profession: "all." Her humiliation was total, and so was her ignorance. She knew she wasn't ready to study with him. She pondered the phrase *"all* you want" for months. What could be better than to be taken seriously? The confidence necessary not to be taken seriously but instead to live as light as a bird and as a feather. What could be better than her husband's love or her students' admiration? Self-love, self-acceptance. What could exceed ten years on her life? A day of gorgeous 20/20 insight. When she saw what was worth fighting for, she was ready to struggle. Later that year, she joined him.

IV

Enlarge the Space in Which
You Can Be Strong

IN THIS MONEY CULTURE, MEN rule the planet from behind big desks. They are lordly, respected, rich. Princessas may want to be like them. But they can never *be* them as long as they try to be *like* them. They can never be powerful as long as they try to be in charge in the same way men take charge.

Practicing men's power only makes you more subject to them, because you can never get as good at it as those born to it. Where does that leave you? Few companies are going to make you CEO. You may learn enough authority skills to command a child or contain a troubled marriage. But are these gains? Or compromises? To "command" or "control" is always a compromise.

History proves that women have failed by fighting men's wars. Women have a place in all the professions, thanks to feminism, but they don't lead in any of them, because they have been fighting much like the powers that be against the powers that be. And when it comes to men, being "like" them isn't strong enough.

Even when we have the advantage, the deck is stacked against us. Look at the biggest scientific project since NASA, the World Wide Web. It is hailed as a feminine structure, a model of communications and relationships, yet not one woman has assumed leadership or ownership of Web companies. Of the hundred new Internet millionaires this year, not one is a woman.

When Rome was sacked, where did the great architects of the empire go? When women have public standing, why do they, like the architects, flee when the barbarians move in? Soon after the flying machine was invented, women claimed a prominent position in the new technology. "Flight became flying," technology guru John Evans has said. "Women took what Wilbur and Orville had invented and transformed the technology of flight into the romance of flying. The skies were packed with aviatrixes who took on the most adventurous routes." But when men got into the game, which they did as soon as there was money to be made in commercial rather than recreational flying, then women gave up. They wouldn't contest men's incursion, as if they feared the exhilaration of power, money, and influence. Flying became disciplined, profitable, and dull. Women pilots all but disappeared for the next fifty years.

Men's power and strategies are based on command-and-control–style systems: someone or some organizing body invents the laws or rules that others are forced to submit to. Rules limit behavior—that's the point of control. The problem is they limit both bad and good behavior. Every woman knows what this feels like: a lover gives you only so much room, insisting on your faithfulness in everything, not just sex; and soon the relationship falters. A doctor, lawyer, or boss says, I support you, but do it my way. A corporation says, Work in this small circle of responsibility day in and day out. It's all command and control, suffocation over freedom.

Women break through the glass ceiling now and then, but not in any way that gives them real power. Among the highest-ranking female Fortune 500 CEOs, one sells Barbie dolls and another's business is in bras and girdles. In all the years since the Industrial Revolution, it's still Barbies, bras, and girdles!

Command-and-control power built a country of dams and roads and huge corporations. But what could this country have been if another style of power had prevailed? What if there had been an alternative to following the laws or breaking the laws: like flaunting them? What if flying *had* dominated flight and women were now running the aviation industry? Would airplanes feel less like bombers? Would flying exhilarate? Would service fit for pashas be routine? Command and control engenders a willed ignorance of possibilities. E. M. Foster personifies this in *Howards End*, in the character of the industrialist Mr. Wilcox. He is having an argument with his wife over the things she says he never notices, "the lights and shades that exist in the greyest conversation." He replies:

> "My motto is Concentrate. I've no intention of frittering away my strength on that kind of thing."
>
> "It isn't frittering away the strength," she protested. "It's enlarging the space in which you may be strong."

Enlarging the space in which to be strong: that is the princessa's goal, no matter what the war. The challenge is to win without first defeating the C&C people—a feat you will learn about in "The Book of Tactics," in the section on "Besting Surpasses Winning" (pages 89–93). But first, the philosophy and strategies of war will demonstrate this: people don't want to be defeated, but they do want to be won—or won over.

V

Femininity Is a Vast Wealth and Deserves to Be Treated as Such

THE PRINCESSA WHO GOVERNS naturally has less and less need to threaten, or to lose. When her power is vested in her tradition—her deep expression of femininity—she is allowed more freedom and excesses than if she tried to impose power.

When all is said and done, Stalin will be remembered as a tyrant who lived during the time of the poet and warrior Anna Akhmatova. She will be honored long after that murderous conquerer is only a memory, in the same way we now read of the sweet struggles Marcus Aurelius had with his conscience rather than of the maraudings celebrated by Julius Caesar. We honor Socrates' battles with his daemon, not Alexander's bloodletting at Persepolis. The conquests of the old conquerers never prevail for long. In these examples, the feminine—not the command-and-control style of struggle—prevails.

Femininity is a vast inheritance, a windfall, and deserves to be treated as such. Vulnerability is one of these riches. Imagine your health fraying, and the black-eyed slit of a CAT scanner swooping over you, staring into your closed eyes and body, seeing you through your good sweater and skin, and pronouncing you slightly damaged goods? The body that has given you so much pleasure—now you'll have to give it back the attention it has never troubled you for. Or imagine your work as responsible for filling every nook and cranny of your self-worth. You lose a client, then another project turns sour. Suddenly everything you learned about your craft seems a lie. You seem a fraud. That is vulnerability. Perhaps you are sitting with your child, both of you at odds over his anger and your determination to contain it. You feel lost because you are striving for control over the situation. You remember your mother's or father's punishing voice filling the room; no matter what, the message comes back at you in full assault. Instead of seeing the inherent power in these situations, and admitting your feelings of weakness, you let these feelings undo you.

It is in this state of powerlessness before your own weakness that you are ready to learn the truth about power. It isn't control, it isn't intimidation. Power is learning from what is inside you. Power, as singer Alanis Morisette said, is "a certain sense of fearlessness about my vulnerability . . . the more truthful and vulnerable I was, the more empowering it was for me."

This is the key to the power of the princessa. You don't control another person; you can only take command of yourself in the situation you find yourself in. That is how you can allow yourself to "let go"—to become outrageous. This is how you can reveal to the enemy your most precious tactics or ideas, this is why you can get closer and closer to him or her rather than try to stay guarded and at a "safe" distance.

What if you tried to read yourself better than a CAT scanner and faced what a lack of control over your body and your world really means? Is your fragility a symptom that you have no power at all? That you have lost control over the thing nearest to you, that is you—your body? Or is a different definition of power at work here? Is your power total freedom to fight as hard as you will because that's what's called for?

Power is the opposite of command and control. Power neither commands nor controls. It marches you into the fray, keeps you open and unarmored in the face of whatever comes: your vulnerability is your power. Your own desires are ultimately more powerful than any designs or traps or attempts at sabotage you may contemplate against the enemy.

Strip away all current ideologies of what power is and you realize that men have always been in awe of women. They have much more power than men. *Power is not what you use. It's what you have.*

Women misidentify power. They mistake it for the

rules of command and control—the law, the mastery, the submission. Misguided, they follow two wrong approaches to power. Either they give up too quickly, or they go overboard and push and push and act like men who try always to dominate, to shut down alternatives in order to gain control. But they aren't men. When they behave like beggars and borrowers of male ways, that creates antagonisms. They don't need to fake it to make clear how able they are.

Imply power. That's the secret. That's the fulcrum by which strategy works: the lever of implied power.

Strength is using the power deep inside you. Not acquired. Not holstered on like a Smith & Wesson. Not advertised by false shows of aggression. Until you are sick, or have your back up against the wall, you may never pay attention to the power deep inside. You may think that what is inside you is buried there because it is not fit to see the light of day, that it is weak and hideous. Somewhere, like most women, you draw a line between the strong and the weak. The strong is the face you present to the world. The weak is the timid response, the occasional tears, the uncertainty, the vulnerability. In a world of men's princely powers, those are liabilities. In the world you now see, they represent power. It is the power of the spy, obvious and hidden at the same time. Only the spy is vulnerable and safe at the same time, detached and present.

Because power is that subterranean and vulnerable, how do you express it?

VI

How to Get People to Act in the Short Run

MACHIAVELLI TAUGHT THE PRINCE the power of oppression. People are childlike; order them about. Tyrannize them. Don't seek love; if they love you, it's a sign you've lost control and they now have the upper hand.

The problem with this kind of power is that you burn up the very sources of energy you are using. The people around you come to hate you. They dream of revenge. In how many marriages is the drama of the Israelis and Palestinians playing itself out, with one side landing a terrorist attack against the other? In the Middle East, the stakes are human lives; in love, the stakes are also human lives.

With Machiavellian control you are in a maintenance position. You maintain only what you already have. At best, you get what others have, but then you must put more and more effort into defending it. Ultimately, you derive fewer and fewer pleasures from all your winnings. You lose the ability to try for the greater winnings possible in a different kind of war game.

Machiavellian power is power of the most primitive kind. The advanced form is a balance of power. Here, the enemy has something you want; in exchange, you give something. The winner is the one who gives away less. This is what it means to have leverage over your opponent. A company gives you some information from which you can infer the longevity of your job, but it withholds the crucial information on how long you will in fact be around. Achieving a balance of power really leads to a kind of insidious war. You think you have won. But the enemy has lulled you into a false peace, has taken the fight out of you.

The most seductive enemy practices a balance-of-power strategy. He keeps seducing you by giving you small wins, or partial information, or carefully metered emotional responses. One minute he is giving, the next withholding, so that you lose all sense of what giving and taking are. Balance of power, like oppression, is also a small game. You trade back and forth only what each of you already has. Each of you feeds on the other's uncertainty: What is he *not* telling me? This increases the uncertainty, and blocks the possibility of a brilliant alliance.

That is why negotiation is useful, but not triumphant. It redistributes what each of you has; it doesn't create a bigger set of possibilities to be won from a battle.

The fears on which these two kinds of power are based make people act according to your wishes in the short run. But only love makes them do things in the long run.

VII

How to Get People to Act in the Long Run

THE STRATEGY AT THE HEART OF the princessa's art is not a menu of alternatives. There is only one strategy, of proven success by all princessas: a combination of love and war. These are not opposites for the princessa. They are the corresponding halves of her single strategy.

To combine love and war requires understanding love in a new light. Love has always been linked to war, but as its antithesis. A soldier would fight his heart out, like Odysseus, and then make the long journey back to his beloved Penelope. So Machiavelli's prince learned that for the sake of power it is better to be feared and respected than loved. Love might compromise his ability to be tough with others. Machiavelli could never imagine that love is the most un-compromising of forces. Love does not need to compromise; to fight from a position of love is to achieve a decisive triumph. The prizes exceed anything the mind expects.

Socrates believed that the lover's brand of war, more than command and control or leverage, is the way to fight. His teacher, Diotima, taught him about the several levels of love, which begin with erotic love and ascend to a pure love of beauty. But she taught him about another kind: public love, or political love. It is a feeling of kinship with every person and object. A blue hinge on a restaurant door stops you with its beauty. A stranger smiles at you as she passes, and though there is no reason for this, you feel her warmth. You feel proud of your country when it triumphs, or of your company when it improves employee well-being. You can trivialize these moments and say these things simply "speak to you." But there is more. That they speak to you at all suggests you are ripely in public love. You are in a mood to see beauty everywhere.

"I feel a solidarity in fate with everything that exists, big or small," said Lou Andreas-Salomé, called the mother of psychoanalysis, the protégée of Freud and the purported lover of two intellectual titans of her time, the poet Rilke and the philosopher Nietzsche. When you feel yourself a part of everything that exists, as if it were placed there for you—even a blue hinge on a door—then nothing seems outside your power. The Machiavellian urge to control hits you when you feel things are outside your control; that's when you want to nail them down.

But when they exist in solidarity with you, your smallest gestures will have tremendous impact. It takes little effort for a princessa to wiggle her toe. If everything is as much a part of her as that toe, she can wiggle the world.

Feel that people are somehow a part of you and something else happens: you become greater than you are individually. Walt Whitman says, "I contain multitudes." The power to fight by love's warring strategy is to know that nothing is outside you or your power, and that you are not limited to the skin and bones and heartbeat you have come to call *you*.

Socrates so believed in this principle of the lover's hold on something greater than reality, something more like a mythic consciousness, that he took this conviction to its utmost. He asked the Athenian senate to abolish its army of trained soldiers and instead recruit lovers to fight Athens's wars. A company of lovestruck troops marching off to battle with stars in their eyes made the plainest sense to him. And who is more fierce than a woman turned tigress when her children are threatened? That is love at war. Who fights harder than a lover scorned? No soldier can strategize as keenly as a lover—the power of her desire alone can force the world to align itself to her dreams. If soldiers could pursue victory with the same determination of lovers pursuing their beloveds, they would win nearly every time on little more than their desire to win. (And if lovers acted strategically, there would be fewer broken hearts.)

A mere kiss provides an example. Myrlie Evers-Williams nearly lost the vote for chairwoman of the NAACP in the early 1990s over fierce objections to her candidacy. When she won by a narrow margin and walked before her detractors to make her acceptance speech, she blew the room a kiss. A kiss is nothing, a bit of breath, no more. It is nothing, but it changes everything. It changed the scene in that room from hostility to respect, even if grudging respect.

A lover is any fighter who believes her desires are shared by the world. A lover feels the sun shines for her. She lives in a dream world where everything is possible. *Love as a strategy is about how to sustain your fighter's dream, in spite of stories people tell about the difference between dream and reality.* Most people live in their dreams but don't make them real. They act as if there is some dividing line between the two. There is none. Montaigne wrote of a woman who lifted a calf every day and was still able to lift it when it became a cow. In her mind, she would always be able to lift this animal, and so she could. This is how the lover's mind remakes reality.

Princessas often get a hint of this early in life. Later, they apply this solidarity to all their relationships, capturing what they love and desire for themselves. Public love becomes part of their visual and emotional vocabulary. They acquire power simply by understanding the existence of love as the best strategy in war.

As a young woman living in London at the end of

the nineteenth century, Gertrude Bell had a taste of this early on. She was reading aloud to her step-mother a story of a hero's death when a knock on the door summoned her to a telegram saying that her lover was dead, the man she'd said good-bye to nine months earlier in terrible grief when her proper Victorian father forbade their marriage. Perhaps part of her felt his death was no coincidence, that there were certain powers lovers had over each other; and then she took this one step further: *If you behaved like a lover with all things, you would have an unusual power over them.* Desire rules the world: say something with conviction and you make it happen. Fight armed with a lover's sensibility (not a nurturer's) and you change the world according to your desires.

Up until the arrival of that telegram, Gertrude had accomplished amazing things—a first at Oxford, among them. She succeeded in conventional terms by taking herself seriously and exceeding all the rules anyone had set down for her, though not her father's dictate that she relinquish her suitor. Now everything changed. She had already been grieving for her lover in his absence; now that grief would be real and complete. If her actions *could* model reality, she would never again take no for an answer. She would not let her negative emotions rule her. She would not say no to any danger or any prohibition. She would express her feelings in the form of public love. Gertrude Bell embarked on the exploits that led to her becoming a world-class adventurer, a reputed spy in Arab countries, a confidante of Lawrence of Arabia, a hero in her own right.

To get people to act in the long run, the princessa understands a mechanism that physicists describe as "strong attractors"—the power of forces that come into direct contact to alter each other. Knowing this changes the rules of the game.

VIII

How One Princessa Aimed High to Meet Her Target

A PRUDENT PRINCESSA ALWAYS follows in the footsteps of her greatest forebears. It is a wise student who proceeds by imitation. But too often we follow the footsteps of those nearest us, in distance and time, and the figures we model ourselves after are not necessarily the best or the noblest, merely the most familiar. We miss the air of greatness possessed by those living in more threatening, perilous times than ours. Aim higher, I say, like a markswoman who knows that she must aim above her target in order to meet her goal.

The story of Magda Trocmé, a French pastor's wife, serves as an outstanding model of a woman who had nothing from fortune—no riches, no great authority—

other than an opportunity to help others. She gave it magnificent form and challenged oppressors and naysayers through a strategy that combined the ways of love and war.

Magda was a World War II resister who knew she could counter any opposing force, no matter how formidable—not by control, not by balance of power, but by this ability to touch others' mythic consciousness. She didn't war against her oppressors; she didn't negotiate with them; she changed the battlefield. She fought reality, or her antagonists' perception of reality. She changed the way they saw reality—their mythic consciousness; she made her dream prevail.

Magda and her husband, André, lived in Le Chambon, a parish in rural Vichy, France. During the Nazi occupation, escaping Jews who fled persecution and certain death were invited into her home for food or a night's rest. Many stayed. Magda did a curious thing. She didn't hide her Jewish refugees. She didn't lock them in a secret annex, as did the rescuers who hid Anne Frank's family. Magda kept her doors open. She talked to her neighbors of the guests in her home. One young escapee, fearing the danger of capture, begged Magda at least to lock the front door. She refused. She said she would not draw a line between the life in her home and the death troops in the streets. A locked door would say to the Nazis, This place is safe, but outside, where you are in command, that is the place of danger. To say that, to announce it, would be to comply with the Nazis' illegitimate power. Perhaps

Magda got away with this because the town was filled with people like her. Perhaps it was because of the power of her belief that she *could* get away with her outrageous stance.

Magda believed that an open door, more than a gun, was a threat to the Nazis, a sign to them that her faith was stronger than their power. If an open door could defy their edicts, what could hundreds of other open doors throughout Europe do? Could women fight the Nazis simply by leaving their doors unlocked? In fact, that is what hundreds of women, leaders of the resistance movement in Sweden, Poland, and Holland, did.

Magda was matter-of-fact about dispersing the tension in her surroundings. Outrageous is what she was, not outraged. A combination of opposites is what she was: passive but resistant, belligerent but unaggressive. A winner who didn't make the enemy feel defeated. A fierce lover, a woman who would not be compromised.

She saved hundreds of Jewish lives and she saved a few German souls too. One night, the Vichy police came to arrest her husband. Word quickly spread that the Germans had rounded up André Trocmé. Dozens of families rushed to the Trocmés' home, setting at André's feet things they would desperately miss but wanted him to have to ease his imprisonment: blankets, bread, tinned meats. The Nazis captors, watching this display as they were trying to haul André off to prison, were shocked by the neighbors' generosity.

Their official hostile facade broke. Four weeks after André's arrest, they found a way to release him.

Once, Magda came home from working at the Cevenol School and found her front door pushed wide open. She walked inside fearfully. She saw that nothing, and no one, had been taken. But something had been left: her home was filled with flowers. She never found out who had done this. "All right," she thought, "let the flowers come in along with the horror."

When you fight the lover's fight, surprises become routine.

Magda set in motion the rules of resistance, the heart of the art of women's war. In traditional male terms, she had no power. She had no armies, no laws on her side. But she knew how to switch the battlefield from the one in which her enemy held all the cards to her own, the one where her reality, her agenda, her desires prevailed.

IX

Tension Disarms Opponents

A PRINCESSA'S GREATEST ALLY IN her war to defend herself or to achieve her desires is her skillful use of tension. Tension is the emotional state that invisibly governs the action in a setting. However, most women, when they sense tension in the air, try to tamp the fire. When the tension is overwhelming women often withdraw, or react in anger, then regret the outburst. They might apologize or compromise. Ordinary women make an effort to get over their anger, as if it were the flu. They cuddle anger out of a child. They resign themselves to a life with demanding parents. They sleep with men to take the war out of them. None of these represent a strategic use of tension. What we experience as tension usually paralyzes us. That is because we let it fill us; we don't use it, fight with it, treat it like a bit of bad weather.

The princessa knows she cannot control others; what she can touch, or influence, is the tension in the room. And this she does, strategically, as smartly as Magda, who opened a door in a world where doors were barricaded, as women living in easier times can unlock their dreams in the face of oppressive forces. By manipulating people's aggressions, fears, assertions of false authority, and other tensions, Magda influenced the town's response to her agenda. She took charge.

A skilled princessa acts in order to build tension. She acts to assume mastery not of other people but over the tension among them.

She opens a meeting by announcing that the news is tough, brace yourselves. She talks about the troubles ahead. Then she switches. She talks of good news, and everyone relaxes in a collective sigh of relief; their bodies go slack, they hear her message in a different way. She may let the tension build again in a few moments, when the emotions in the room have had their moment of respite. She might increase and decrease the tension a few more times. Her use of tension is subtle; only the effect is dramatic.

In Shakespeare's *Julius Caesar*, Mark Antony's oration at Caesar's funeral skillfully uses tension to raise the emotions of the crowd, to incite rebellion against Caesar's murderers. Mark Antony tells the crowd that he doesn't want to stir them up; so they relax, the better to hear the things he then says to stir them up. He says he is a plain and blunt man, but only to keep them from suspecting the artistry—or artifice—of his speech. Self-contradiction can be a valuable vehicle for creating tension. "Do I contradict myself? Very well then I contradict myself," wrote Walt Whitman. Mark Antony calms in order to excite; he makes himself small to build himself up. Magda did the same; she left her doors open not to fight, but to show there was no point in fighting. She defused the Nazis' power, along with the citizens of Le Chambon; they were aware of the danger but refused to compromise their lives and beliefs.

The use of tension disarms opponents; more important, it makes them react to you. Use contradictions. Find the prevailing sentiment or law in any situation and act as if it were cast not in stone but in sand. When a princessa appreciates how she herself is a combination of opposite characteristics—ferocity and tenderness, openness and determination—and doesn't struggle for consistency, she will find it easier to address the opposing tensions in a confrontation.

Cordelia tells her father, King Lear, that she loves him, not the way flowers adore the sun but "according to my bond." These are drier words than Lear, the old sentimentalist and control artist, wants to hear from his beloved youngest daughter. She demands nothing of her father—no money, no security. But in fact she asks for more than he can give: that he understand her. Cordelia's words may be cold, but her love is deep and sincere. She raises her father's expectations, telling him no one could love him more. Then she flattens those expectations with all her talk about her duties to Lear and her filial obligations. It is her effort to get Lear to understand her on her terms. Her sisters, Regan and Goneril, tell him exactly what he wants to hear, praise him to the skies, to extract the maximum inheritance.

Cordelia, like Magda, violates the laws of common understanding. Her use of tension leaves the old king uncertain. He entrusts himself to the care of his apparently loving older daughters and banishes Cordelia for her insolence. But her words fight for her. Though she leaves the stage, her presence directs everything. Tension has established Cordelia as a figure of enormous, mythic authority.

Cordelia speaks only ninety-one lines in Shakespeare's great tragedy, but her influence is never absent. This is the mark of the princessa who has learned her true power. *When your absence has the authority of your presence, that is power.* Eventually Lear realizes the truth—that Cordelia was sincere and his other daughters false.

Tension is the fulcrum to use. It will open, disarm, and unsettle your opponent. It will give you the edge, the means past his defenses. By these means you touch the mythic consciousness of another, or others. Tension is so effective because it matches the rhythm of the heartbeat, which is the same as any mesmerizing primal rhythm—the one-two, taut-relaxed, blunt-soft beat. In a tough situation, a skillful use of tension allows you to play with a crowd's heartbeat, its life, its breath. Using tension gets you under another's skin, where their defenses are weakest.

Tension comes in many forms. It is not just your words, but the timing of your words. If you are up against an enemy who is bullying you, talking loudly and harshly and issuing directives, disarm him by speaking slowly, and softly. He will almost hypnotically adapt himself to your rhythms. He will slow down, not just his voice but also his demands. If, on the other hand, your opponent is ensnarling you in a process you must hurry along, then talking faster will speed him up. Tension is also expressed in a host of other weapons—in the symbols of power, dress, sex. You will read about these in more detail in "The Book of Subtle Weapons," beginning on page 127.

Scheherazade played with tensions. She had a strategy for saving the kingdom's young girls, who were dying in epidemic numbers. Each night a new virgin was summoned to the sultan's chambers for one night of lovemaking, then killed at daybreak lest she go on and betray him. Scheherazade's strategy for stopping the murders was outrageous. She volunteered to be the sultan's next sacrifice. After lovemaking, she began telling a story, which he overheard, and heated things up again. Her story walked a narrative path of conflict and resolution. She continued her tale until the sultan fell asleep. The next day, he couldn't bear to behead her; he had to hear the rest of her story. Stories and lovemaking—tension and release—saved Scheherazade's life and after 1,001 nights won her the sultan's love and his trust.

X

Four Kinds of Strategic Tension

CONFRONTATION, REMEMBER, IS A form of relationship. It is one of the few relationships where power is expressed, not hidden. To enter into a confrontation in which you can prevail, identify the kinds of tension—let's call them energies—already present.

All tension of a strategic kind is governed by four principles. They:

1. Intensify feelings
2. Incite others toward a big goal or cause
3. Invalidate and refuse to accept predominant beliefs
4. Engage in blocking or slowing down

Each of these focuses the action in ways that give you influence over it. Let's study them a bit closer.

To *intensify* feelings, let everything sink deep inside you. Don't protect yourself from the pain you feel or see around you. Or from your desires. Provoke the same in others, both supporters and opponents. You need to feel the importance, the excitement, the plausibility of your mission. If you don't feel it, no one else will. Magda did this by defying the Nazis' power; she didn't protect herself from the refugees' fears—she shared them. Cordelia did this by playing forcefully on Lear's desire to be loved, which she shared. For the basic tactics on how to do this in your wars, see "The Eighteen Tactics of the Great Warrior Princessas" (pages 98–125), particularly tactics one, two, and three in a conflict's early stages, when you need to boost your strength and commitment to fight. Later, in the heat of battle, tactics fifteen, sixteen, and seventeen bring you to the point at which you—your feelings (but not your ego)—are driving the action.

To *incite* others, choose the biggest possible goal to fight for. People fight with you when they care about the battle. Make a war too small and it's yours alone; no one will join in the action. When Rosa Parks refused to move to the back of the white man's bus, she didn't complain about her individual rights. Her personal struggle was symbolic of a bigger war for freedom and civil rights. Anna Akhmatova's poems in defiance of Stalin's repression focused on what kind of people the victors of war would be—not on who would win, not on whether she herself would have bread and a warm room, but whether the winners would be decent, worthy people, and any better morally and emotionally than the tyrannical losers. Hers was a bigger goal by far than just winning. See tactics four, five, and six.

To *invalidate* the predominant authority, do not react to it. He who bears the trappings of authority doesn't necessarily own authority. Behave as if you know that authority, for all the fear he, she, or it inspires in others, has no governance over you. A boss controls only your current job, he doesn't control you. This is vital, because if he behaves outlandishly, realize you can resist him. Gandhi won his war for freedom from the tyrannical rule of the British Army by invalidating the power of the Army. How he did it is the subject of tactics seven, eight, nine, and ten.

Blocking means that you act in order to deter the authority's progress away from his or her own goals. There are various ways to stop an opponent so that you have the opportunity to push your desires. You ask a lot of questions. You talk slowly. You see yourself as a line of defense the opponent must get through to achieve his or her aims. That is how you come to take charge. In the theater, directors "block" the movements of the actors, deciding exactly where they will stand, sit, enter, and exit. They do this strategically, knowing full well that movement is as important as language. Women who think that merely discussing a problem will solve it are wrong. Language at any volume can be too "quiet." Movement is a language. Often, movement triggers emotion, not vice versa. The princessa directs another's action through the subtlety of her tactics. She knows that if she stands in a certain way, in a certain proximity, or moves with a specific speed, she determines her opponent's emotions and behavior. People pick up each other's rhythms; they're often the hardest element to resist. Influencing the physical agenda in any confrontation is therefore as important as what you say. The tactics that apply to blocking are twelve, thirteen, and fourteen.

These four principles of tension have at their heart the method of resistance. Not defiance, not subterfuge, not charm, but standing against. That is literally what resistance means: *standing*—or holding your ground—*against* the opponent, the person or point of view that has you stuck. Resistance is the opposite of compromise, negotiation, nurturance. *It means not fighting the enemy's war or anything like a traditional war of two clashing parties. It means luring the enemy into fighting on your ground, into your battle, where you command the action.*

Resistance works like this:

You are locked in a struggle with an attacker or opponent who is stronger than you. The easiest thing to do is to push back. The harder course is to stop struggling. It's harder because fight or flight is the natural response to most attacks. But if you stop struggling when an attacker grabs you by the shoulders, the chances are good that he will helplessly fall straight into your lap. To stop struggling does not mean that you stop fighting. It means that you fight by resisting.

Resistance in battle is much like resistance in the human body. A healthy organism fights an attacking virus by producing antibodies against it. The body transforms the attacker into a source of new strength, not weakness. Antibodies neutralize it, much as Magda neutralized the Nazis. Resistance is a source of power that is akin to beauty. Wind pouring through a reed sounds hollow—unless the reed contains resistances, as a flute contains chambers, which turn the air into music.

The four principles of tension are like the chambers in a flute. They turn the breath of your fearlessness and determination into notes. One princessa was having a terrible time trying to win the attention of a client she badly wanted to impress. How would he notice her? What could she say?

Without realizing it, she was making him the enemy by exaggerating his importance. She tried for weeks to draft a letter introducing herself and her services. Every attempt seemed to her more inadequate than the last. With every failure, he became bigger in her eyes—more formidable, more remote. And she became smaller and more hopeless.

My advice to her was to use resistance: "Don't fight yourself. Use the angst you feel as your means of approaching him. Be truthful. Tell him this letter is the last page in a whole book of letters you've written him in the past month. That none seemed good enough to send. The ambition you bring to his career would be the perfect match for his own ambitions. That's why you hope he'll meet you to hear more.''

When the enemy is the princessa herself, she can play the resister to her own fears. In this case, the princessa changed the nature of the war with herself. She fell, so to speak, into her own lap.

This woman used *intensification* (she emphasized her angst) and *incitement* (she made her potential client a collaborator and ally when she told him his standards inspired her drive for perfection); she *invalidated* his overwhelming authority (by sending the letter, she created an approachable figure of this towering icon) and engaged in *blocking* (she set herself up as his opposite and his equal, or better-than-equal, coming at him boldly, though unknown and untested, from out of the blue).

Her newfound skill, the resister's skill, also served her in love. What we do in work, we do in love. Although we are taught otherwise, we are the same person in both arenas, so the resister's strategy works every bit as effectively. Once she realized she didn't have to fight her weakness—her only enemy, in this case—she became bold, venturesome. She found herself becoming more of a guiding force in her new marriage. The spirit spilled over into all the arenas of her life.

XI

The Paradox of Power Anorexia

THE THING THAT STANDS BETWEEN many women and the ability to get what they want is a proclivity toward self-denial.

We have all seen this self-denial manifested in our behavior toward food and appetite, and in its most extreme form in the disorder anorexia. But anorexia is a symptom of a deeper aspect of self-denial: a preference for powerlessness. This is the disorder power anorexia.

A power anorexic gives off identifiable signs. She has an emotional frailty. She is readily agreeable and can barely manage a "no" even when the prevailing atmosphere is one of kindness. She shrugs off compliments. She says "No thanks, I'll do it myself" when others try to help her. She studies people in power, looking to them for approval. Outfits of black and beige fill her closet, colors of mourning and camouflage. She is adverbially dependent. Words like "very" and "really" are always on her tongue. She says, "This is really very, very good," as if her opinion accounts for so little she must overemphasize it.

She also undermines her conversation by peppering it with exaggerated exclamations, or else she fails to speak up even when she knows her idea will solve the problem. She snatches defeat from the jaws of victory. She fears losing so badly she stops trying to win. She doesn't study her defeats as possible failures of strategy; she ignores them. Most poisonously, she is harder on herself than any enemy could ever be. With each display of power anorexia, she grows thinner and more inconsequential in her eyes and others'. She has no weight, no substance, no presence.

Princessas must eat to put fat on their character.

A princessa doesn't say no to herself. She doesn't fade into the shadows when she should make herself formidable and noticed. Joan of Arc wore white into battle in order to look big and obvious. Not so she would get shot, but just the opposite. An enemy who sees that you cannot be intimidated is not likely to try to intimidate you.

Self-denial, pencil-thinness, a position on the sidelines—none of these afford power.

A friend told me of her recent dream about Jackie

Onassis. Jackie turned to my friend with a big welcoming smile. My friend was shocked; in the years since she died, Jackie had gotten chubby. Suddenly back, she grabbed my friend's arm and they walked up Broadway together like an old married couple. A glassware vendor saw them, and rushed to give Jackie samples of his work. She accepted his gifts. He offered her his skis, and she took these too—*why* my friend couldn't understand. She must have skis, this woman thought. Why didn't she say no? Jackie's arms were full now. "Let me put these away," she said, and disappeared into a Manhattan high-rise. My friend waited for hours in the lobby, but Jackie didn't come back down. When she woke up, her greatest horror wasn't that Jackie had abandoned her but that her icon had gotten fat in goddess heaven.

How could she, so self-aware in life, a woman who would cut her food into the tiniest bite-size pieces so no photographer would catch her with a wad of food in her cheek, how could she let herself go? Even in a dream? That was my friend's first thought. Her second was relief: Jackie wasn't denying herself anything anymore. But that was only half true. In fact, Jackie had denied herself very little in life. She'd always done just what she wanted. She claimed the world stage as aggressively as her husband, the President. She married Aristotle Onassis despite the public outrage. She took a job in publishing because she loved the intellectual stimulation. What former First Lady had ever accepted a paycheck, walked to work, eaten in the company cafeteria? Dante saw that death burns off illusions, that finally a person appears exactly as he or she is. My friend realized that Jackie was always "chubby," though she had never seen it before. Jackie in life didn't work at being pencil-thin—an active life made her skinny. She didn't work at keeping experience at a safe distance. She could accept strangers' gifts, even things she didn't need, allowing herself to feel bestowed. This was the message of my friend's dream, meant for her: Deny your hunger and you deny your self, you deny your strength.

To eat is to take, to make public your need and your dependence. To eat is to learn to be selfish. There is even more power when self-sufficiency and self-reliance leave you, when you realize you do need, and want, and can take. And that what you take—your quarry—is made of the same stuff as you. Nothing is foreign. Nothing is what you "deserve"—*the things you want are the things you need*. Whatever you can assimilate you can make part of your character, and fatten it.

The princessa has a different relationship to the world than most women. She thinks of herself as a hunter. She feels the world is there to feed her. She knows she may take, that she has the right to grow big on her desires.

She knows that to nourish herself is to take responsibility. When she takes, she is sure she wants what she can have, that she can eat it all, that she will waste none of it. A job, a love, a compliment: assimilate them deep into your marrow as if they are yours by the divine right of being alive.

Life will provide for you the way it provides for the hunter. You won't need to feel desperate when you know deep down that there will always be a meal. Trust the future to feed you.

Know there is no taking from the world without giving back. Eat in order to give. Mother Meera, an Indian mystic, eats rapaciously, in this way: During her evening darshans, or healing sessions, visitors bow down before a seated "Ma" to let her cradle their head. She places her finger on either side of each visitor's head. The visitor feels the heat leave Ma's fingers and burn into his or her head. Ma closes her eyes and meditates. But if you were to watch her, you would see her swallowing and swallowing. She is eating the bad in you and in the world. A powerful woman eats the bad with the good. She doesn't protect herself from either. She is open and unarmored, strange though this state is for a warrior. She does this not in order to be strong *but because she is strong;* this eating reminds her of that fact.

Don't refuse anything.

✦

HISTORICALLY, MEN'S GREATEST tyranny over women has centered on their bodies: the tyranny over reproductive rights, the tyranny of thinness and fashion and objectification. We will never be strong if we don't eat, if we don't give our bodies some freedom, if we allow others to objectify us or we continue to objectify ourselves. It's a war. Following are the tactics and weapons necessary for the fight.

THE BOOK OF *Tactics*

⚜

First they ignore you, then they
ridicule you, then they fight you,
and then you win.
—Gandhi

I

Besting Surpasses Winning

❧ MOST WOMEN CANNOT WIN. NOT
because a woman cannot fight strategically. But
because no one wants her to win, and often neither
does she. Both she and her opponents see to it that she
fails. She herself may become consumed with guilt if
she wins—guilt for having created another's loss. Men
hate losing to a woman; this can prompt a counterat-
tack. And to another woman, a triumphant woman is
a lifelong threat.

To get what you want, you must win. But because
winning is so threatening, the best way to win is *to
best*.

Machiavelli's prince could destroy his opponents
and be secure in his triumph. Sun Tzu could play foot-

sie with his enemy and humiliate him with his ingenuity. But the princessa cannot cripple the enemy. She must make her opponent an unwitting ally. This means neither hurting him nor eroding his confidence. Besting leaves the opponent—the loser—unhurt and inspired. Besting is a win in which you overcome an antagonist in high style. It suggests winning by achieving the best, as in an Olympic performance where an athelete's best score—your winning score—does not rob the losers of their dignity. It offers a clear and inspiring new record, a new level in performance, which motivates everybody.

For the princessa, who is always fighting a come-from-behind war, besting is the only way to win because it means winning with a losing hand. Anyone can win with a winning hand. Only the princessa can win with less.

Inanna, a Sumerian princess, was a princessa who became an expert at besting. If she were alive today, she would be the entrepreneur who wants a piece of the action, a lover who wants to be understood, a young woman sitting at supper before a father who metes out special punishment to her because she defies his orders to listen to and not question her parents. The princessa knows she embodies all the women of myth; she enacts their conflicts at one time or another in her own life. Inanna's story will be yours when you try to take any of the powers or pleasures or promotions another is hoarding. Inanna succeeded by besting the authority of authorities—the king, her father.

Inanna's story opens like that of the Buddha. She leaves her father's castle to journey into the real world. Outside, she is amazed by what she sees: people everywhere in poverty, misery, and pain. She realizes the world suffers because her father has been hoarding all the beauties of the world—the holy *me*, the powers of poetry, celebration, happiness, and beauty. As long as she lives in her father's castle, she enjoys these things. Outside, there is nothing to live for. Inanna at this point is any woman who determines she wants more than her given lot in life. Like any hero, she must act to change this; she sees she must become self-reliant, which is the heroic awakening.

Any other means would fail her: she cannot negotiate with her father to release the *me*; she has nothing to give him of equal value. She cannot demand these powers; he would laughingly dismiss her. She cannot fight him for control of the *me* in any conventional sense, for she has no armies of support. She does the one thing she can do: she decides to best her father.

She makes a date to have dinner with him. She herself waits upon him. She serves him with her own two hands. She keeps his glass filled with wine. As he drinks, she empties hers into the thirsty earth. She charms him with her wit, this daughter of his; her attentions delight him. She challenges him to a game of chess, and he agrees to play. "What do you want to play for?" he asks her. "Bet the holy *me*," she says. He is impressed by her beauty, her moxie, and he is certain she stands no chance against him. He agrees to the game. She beats him again and again. He cannot keep up with her, because of the drink and his own blind belief in himself. Inanna grabs the holy *me*, jumps into a boat, and on the other side of the river, releases the powers into the world. Her father cannot stop her. When he comes to, he sees that while she has taken his prize possessions, she has made the world more beautiful than it was, and he himself need not be confined to the castle anymore.

This is besting. By her own clever means, Inanna has won for herself and for all around her.

Gandhi similarly bested the British overlords. Rather than conceive a simple win against them, he used the tactics described in the next chapter to triumph over them in such a way that they, too, could only be impressed by the fight itself and could benefit from his win.

But the best tale of besting is what happened to the winningest general in history at the hands of twelve princessas.

Legend has it that Sun Tzu was being feted for his string of brilliant victories when he boasted that there was no one he couldn't transform into a brilliant warrior. No one? the emperor asked. Even my beautiful concubines? Even them, Sun Tzu insisted. And so the very next morning Sun Tzu assembled the twelve women in the royal courtyard and began instructing them in the basics of marching. He lined them up and barked his orders. The concubines thought it ridiculous to stand together like rooted trees, or to pay attention to a fool shouting "hup." They collapsed in giggles. They got up and walked around as they desired. After a morning of not the slightest success, Sun Tzu went before the emperor and, humiliated, admitted his failure. He said the concubines were too stupid to learn war skills. What he never realized was that their besting skills had handed him his first and only defeat.

II

How Besting Is Accomplished

❦ ALL GREAT GENERALS KNOW THAT
while ancient battles were won with superior
weapons or forces, modern battles are won by ideas.
The more outrageous the idea, the better the chances
of winning. It was Gandhi's outrageous notion that
he, with no guns or money, could break the back
of the British Empire. It was Magda's outrageous
belief that she was more powerful than her oppressors. And Dian Fossey's outrageous notion was that
she could make the poachers murdering the gorillas in
her camp believe she was a goddess—something
she did one night when she built up her fire into a
bonfire and began throwing dollar bills into it.
The greedy poachers couldn't believe anyone but a

higher force would take so irreverent an approach to their god.

Such ideas—strategies—were the subject of "The Book of Strategy," where the warriors all had more than an idea; they had brilliant tactics to guide them in expressing the idea. As artists know form and color, princessas must know tactics. So Magda flung open the doors to her home; Dian fed a flame with dollar bills; Gandhi told the British that not even an atom bomb would stop him. He said, "I will not go underground, I will not go into shelter. I will come out in the open and let the pilot see I have not a trace of evil against him. The pilot will not see our faces from his great height, I know. But that longing in our hearts— that he will not come to harm—would reach up to him and his eyes would be opened." That is a tactic— an action designed to provoke a favorable counteraction in the opponent. And it is a particular kind of tactic—that of besting: demonstrating to the opponent that your win is also his win. The princessa's tactics must model a new behavior for her enemy to follow. Once he models his behavior on hers, he will find his aims converging on one agenda—hers. Their eyes, as Gandhi said, "would be opened."

Model in your behavior what you want to see in the enemy. Hillary Clinton's strategies failed because the tactics she followed prompted nothing better in her enemies. Hillary is a role model to a great many women. Yet she made a number of mistakes that diminished her influence. Her mistakes stand in opposition to the tactics of besting. For example, when she was the First Lady of Arkansas, she focused so much critical attention on a rival senator whose work had been largely obscure, it was said that she "created" him. She didn't like his views, and she didn't care for him personally, so she pounded away at his mistakes and problems in interviews. As a result, he rose to national attention and became an even more vicious and effective enemy of hers. Since then, she has been careful to keep her distance from enemies.

The princessa behaves in exactly the opposite way. *She knows she needs proximity to the enemy in order to build her enemy's strengths. She doesn't fear her enemy's strengths; she uses them.*

In another tactical error, Hillary Clinton was so determined to win her health care package that she made too many autonomous moves, believing she could prevail if she kept in control of the situation. Ultimately, she needed to be reined in, and her husband's team was dispatched to work against her. The princessa, on the other hand, *makes a war hers, but not to the exclusion of others. She makes her war others' war too.*

Hillary also believed she would prevail if she kept her opponents on the ropes. But the princessa's style is not to box people in; rather, it leaves room for them to change their minds. *Princessas believe that today's enemy is tomorrow's ally.*

Aides say Hillary is very sure of herself and does not want to revisit issues that have been decided. That sureness about her own judgment is a profound weakness. The princessa is always willing to reconsider strategies, listen to dissenting voices.

Hillary fought like a prince, and fought to conquer rather than to best. Success lies elsewhere.

III

The Eighteen Tactics of the Great Warrior Princessas

 THE TRUTH OF WORDS AND IDEAS is in their action.

Tactics are "actions towards results." Strategy is the *why*, and tactics are the *how*, of the princessa's plan. Most wars, as noted, are won by outrageous ideas. But ideas are expressed in action, where the gringa fighter is usually at her weakest. A woman may be active and busy but know little or nothing about pure action— about the kind of specific, sculpted behavior meant to advance her agenda, not simply complete a task.

Gandhi used to say that God appears not in person but in action. True for God, and true for the princessa. No one, and certainly no enemy, can know you apart from your most creative actions. He won't know your ideas; he won't be won over by what you think unless you know how to translate what you think not merely into words but into action. Unless you reveal it.

Women have internalized so much failure that they often lapse into psychological crisis and are afraid to act. The power in the following actions or tactics—all of them besting tactics—build on the power you have. As tactics go, these are not big, sweeping actions, like deploying forces or setting traps. They are precise maneuvers. They don't necessarily require any great effort to produce a desired impact. They are more than simple steps. Steps are formulaic, predictable, carried out by rote. Anyone can follow the steps of a recipe and create a dish. Creating something unique involves a different kind of plan altogether, combining the determination of a brave pioneer, the innovation of a free thinker, and the outlook of a visionary.

Think of these tactics as rituals. Unlike steps, rituals do not control the action; they provoke it into following certain directions. Ritual literally means "to go, run, let flow." Become acquainted with the rituals on the succeeding pages. Use what you know about the princessa's larger-than-life character, about the way of seeing called spying, about the principles of tension, about the nature of resistance. What you have learned as ideas you will now be able to express in action.

The eighteen rituals of action I will describe make a princessa an actualist, not an activist. She cares about making her opinions *true in action*. She makes herself real and true in all components of her life. The eighteenth ritual, the most challenging of them, is described in the next chapter.

Follow these rituals and no one, no authority, will look down upon you. They will look you in the eye.

One
Think through the body

Imagine yourself a human shield rather than a sword. Your mind will operate to deflect the opponent's anger, hostility, malign intent. In Elaine Scarry's words, think *through* the body.

Golda Meir was thought of as the "Iron Hand." Margaret Thatcher was considered the "Iron Lady." They didn't yield. They stood firm. Firmness begins with how you see yourself. As the resistant body, you are a passive weapon. Poet Judy Grahn salutes the first woman warrior, Queen Boadicea:

> *I am the wall at the lip of the water*
> *I am the rock that refused to be battered.*

Think of the body in these images, as a line of resistance. Let the assault stop before it reaches you. A Palestinian woman, told she must identify herself in public documents as Israeli, said, "But I am Palestinian. My hair is Palestinian, my body is Palestinian, and the words I speak are Palestinian." Make the body a constant source of freshly invented obstructions.

Two
Abandon all notions of a tit-for-tat fight

There is no such thing as revenge in this game. Not even the idea that revenge is a dish best served cold.

In this war, you will *not* give as good as you get. You will give no apparent fight at all.

Gandhi called this tactic ahimsa, which means refusing to harm others. It means not responding in kind. Even in your mind, you don't dare your opponent. You don't threaten. You don't think, Hurt me, and I'll get back at you. Ahimsa is the "strength that is akin to cowardice."

Three
Behave as if your enemy is your ally

Do the unexpected. Be tenderly alert to your enemy's vulnerabilities. When Gandhi spoke of standing in the open while a bomber flew overhead, he was in fact claiming that he felt safer than the pilot, who had to be protected by tons of war machine. Gandhi was protected by his convictions, which were much stronger and would outlast any hatred. He was right.

You have great influence over a colossal opponent. Tell a lover he has a strong and generous character, behave as if he does without criticism and anger at his difficult ways, and you will model that behavior in him. Strength and generosity will become more prominent features of his character. People rise to heroic expectations of them. The bigger your expectations— not your demands, please note—the harder others try to achieve them. The difference is that expectations are expressed in love; demands are said in anger.

Recognize that your enemy or opponent is himself oppressed by a bigger foe. Appealing to the common enemy teaches him to relax his antagonism. And encouraging his heroism turns this foe into a collaborator.

Four

Create a "monster mesh"

Build a network of support. Convince the enemy that opposition is a loss for you and a bigger loss for him. Do this by creating a mesh of support. A mesh is hard to attack because its strength is spread widely. Mexico's Zapatista rebels talk a lot more than they fight. When attacked, they turn to their network of friends and groups interested in the same matters. They patch together a lobby. They don't need an army. They need only to share an idea or ideology that matters to a lot of people.

Call on people to help. Make sure others know what you stand for. Encourage others to question your aims, because people who question you will soon question themselves—and this is a valuable state of affairs when you want to change others' thinking to fit your agenda. You want them to think about you as much as possible so that you become the embodiment of your idea. Once they arrive at the question "Who is she?" they are finally taking you seriously. They are no longer detached; they are that much closer to seeing the world through your eyes. Do this again and again, with as many people as possible, and you will have created a great deal of support. See also the example of Melanie Klein (see pages 150–51), who built a monster mesh of supporters and antagonists alike, which drove her ideas onto a larger stage.

Five
Become more like the enemy than the enemy

Adopting his position shocks the enemy. What you gain from doing so is much more effective than anything you ever accomplish by holding firm to your position. This tactic is valuable when you face an entrenched enemy who just appears to be getting stronger, no matter what you do. A quick change, a shock to everybody's system, is in order.

A freedom-loving rock group in Eastern Europe called Laibach had an ingenious solution to what seemed an unwinnable situation. The party they favored had been voted out of office. Instead of reacting by warring against the new dictators, Laibach began acting like the despots themselves. They started by appearing to define their enemy as their friend. They praised tyrants; they adopted the very agenda they had once protested. It would be tantamount to a manager suddenly becoming more bossy than any of her tyrannical bosses. The sudden change had great impact.

In the case of Laibach, everyone started asking, What happened? Supporters and dictators alike grew confused by Laibach's change in tactics. Had Laibach changed their stripes?

No. Laibach knew that a stance of angry revolt against whatever big enemy you are fighting only shores up the power structure. When a woman fights against "white male oppression," white males become only stronger and more resistant. You reinforce—or model—the hated behavior by your anger and demands. Defiance makes your enemy hold more tightly to his position than resistance does. Complaints do not change the battle space. Polarization forces each side to positions of greater hostility.

Instead, behave like the people you hate, and be even more like the hated than they are themselves. So Laibach, by means of their elusiveness and ambiguity—had they or had they not joined the other side?—compelled people to take up their own individual positions. In questioning Laibach's allegiance, people began to think for themselves. Laibach brought people around to the point where, democratically, they decided their own fate. Laibach's ultimate cause—freedom—got a new burst of support.

Six
Reduce the conflict to its bare essentials

Seeing the essentials of any situation helps you discard costly defenses and denials and brings you closer to realizing the hidden potentials of goodwill and energetic deeds. Use the tactics of the Five Whys to reveal the concealed. Become the spy. Strip away ego, jealousy, self-righteousness. The truth is simple, unfettered, clear. Let it be your guide.

You will feel a lightness, a joy at such moments when you can reduce the conflict inherent in any relationship, business or personal, to its bare essentials. It's as if you have become godlike and can float above the turmoil to see it clearly for what it is.

Seven
Oppose power, don't fight it directly

Rely on the tactic of As If.

Act *as if* the power you seek *is already yours*. Magda did so with the Nazis. She acted *as if* the Nazi edicts had no force over her. And so her antagonists came to believe they didn't. Gandhi did not directly fight the British; he opposed their edicts and acted *as if* the people of India, long cowed by submission to authority, in fact had full power, had already won freedom, and merely had to get the British to acknowledge this.

Nor did Martin Luther King, Jr., do outright battle with the white establishment. Each opposed power (1) by disbelieving in the "prevailing" power, and (2) by believing "their side" had already won—and it was only left to make the win a matter of public record.

Instead of acceding to the television producer who wanted to offer another person the job a princessa had her heart set on, she began behaving *as if* the on-camera job were already hers. She called a meeting with the producer and spoke about how she planned to handle the first show, about those she would invite as guests, and so on. At first the producer was stupefied by her brazenness. He was so shocked by the spectacle that he listened. Then, as she went on spinning her scenario, he began to see that, improbable as it all seemed, she had a handle on how to run things, a better handle than he—or his "ideal" candidate—had. By the end of the meeting, he was on his way to being persuaded that she was the best person for the job. Remember that desire rules: when you behave as if you already have your desires, you convince others you already have them too.

Eight
Study every situation for its opposite

Power always contains the seeds of its own weakness and instability. That is the key to reversing anyone's or anything's hold over you. Contradict rather than confront the governing power, and the dispersal of power lets you rise.

Ask yourself, What is my enemy's greatest strength? In that strength lies the weakness you will target. If the enemy's greatest strength is speed, go for quality.

An attacker who comes at you with all the force of his or her power physical or organizational, can be defused if you don't struggle against strength. While the enemy expends energy fighting, you will be gaining strength.

You are in a meeting where the power is dominated by X. She is overbearing and is ruining the meeting. She is attacking your skills. Go to the opposite extreme. Don't defend yourself. Instead, recommend a different course of action. Play her scenario out. Once X sees that you are openminded, she will no longer feel up against the wall. But you'll have her just where you want her, and she won't even know it. Or deflect her power by inviting others in the room into the discussion. Shift the center of attention, invite others to take part, and you defuse the source of overweening power.

Play every strength (even weaknesses) and you have power.

Nine
Be ready to get hurt and yet not inflict hurt

Never exact revenge. That only strengthens the enemy.

Instead, be vulnerable. Machiavelli counsels the prince to lie to others and keep the truth to himself. His point is to put the enemy on the defensive, which he defines as uncertainty.

Therefore: Be true in a context where everyone is hidden. Be open when everyone else is armored. Accept when everyone else is rejecting. Be determined not to violate another person's essence, for such antagonism can invoke only counterantagonism, which may end in truce but not in truth, and therefore not in a victory for you. Respect the truth in another person.

You could get hurt. You will get hurt. But in a confrontation in which you show openness, a hurt is less painful than when you are self-protected. Just as in a fall, you're better off loosening up than steeling yourself against impact. When the enemy sees how exposed you make yourself, he knows you are in the fight for keeps; he knows you are not bluffing. This is different from accepting a victim's role and taking blows; the victim has no goal of her own. The readiness to be hurt in action when you have a target and are moving toward it shows strength; the readiness to be hurt in a passive stance is suicidal.

Never exact revenge, or penance, or make your opponent believe he "has it coming to him." This implicates you in a mixture of pride and guilt that undermines your position, psychologically and ethically.

George Eliot, often called the female Shakespeare, was widely shunned by her contemporaries for living with her lover, George Lewes. Yet she "did not fight against the restrictions imposed upon her. Rather, she quietly built a meaningful life around them."

While unimaginable today, an unmarried couple in Victorian England was all but burned at the stake. George Eliot was condemned as untrustworthy, a home wrecker, unscrupulous. She resolved to take the attacks the way a fighter takes blows. Because her attackers' comments did not trouble her, she knew they weren't true. And because their comments did not trouble her, her attackers also caught on that they were not true.

Meanwhile, she wrote novels meant as moral education, fighting her mean-spirited, small-minded opponents from her own heightened ground. It proved a good tactic. As a young woman, she was thought to be unbelievably ugly (her first suitor, Herbert Spencer, told her friends he could not bring himself to marry her for her lack of beauty). But after she ignored attacks against her morals and her looks, and fought her own wars, men and women traveled the world over to see George Eliot, the novelist and saint, moralist and teacher. Some claimed she was the most beautiful woman they had ever laid eyes on.

Ten
Let something new enter to destroy a boundary

Introduce something new or surprising or unfamiliar into the picture and you erode an opponent's conviction.

Don't reject things, like new ideas, or new colleagues; welcome everything into a project. Every new person, idea, situation, favors the person who expects them, and most people don't.

Gertrude Stein paid tribute to this point of view. "Everything must come into your scheme," she said of the creative life; "otherwise you cannot achieve real simplicity."

She herself built a career on this advice. "One of the remarkable features of her career was its resiliency," according to historian James Mellow. "Out of curiosity, plain affection, and an extremely shrewd understanding of how to conduct a career in the modern world, Gertrude cultivated the young in every generation. At the beginning of the century, she promoted the vanguard of artists of Paris; in the twenties, she took on young writers, journalists, publicists, and the editors of the little magazines that had, as she was fond of quoting, 'died to make verse free'; in the thirties, she sought out a new crop of admirers by lecturing college and prep-school students during a much publicized American tour; in the forties, she adopted, wholesale, the American GIs of World War II—thus providing herself with a perennial audience"—constant support, constant admiration.

Enlarge your life, your circle, your mind. Boundaries do more than keep others out; they lock you in.

Eleven
Conduct your campaign entirely in the open and at close range

Say what you want (rather than name your grievance or hurt). Declare also how you intend to get it.

In the wars of intimacy, the one who shares information triumphs over the information holder. This is as true for your behavior with enemies as with allies. You are better off spreading information about your aim and tactics than withholding it or sending out decoys. Forget about hiding things. "Information is like a rose, it grows thorns in your heart," said spy and World War II resister Mary Lindell. Information you hold close to you disables you.

Say the truth and act the truth. If you tell an opponent what he wants to hear, not what you mean, you become a manipulator—a woman who has grown content with small gains. Tell people what you think they want to hear and you ultimately convey that you are a coward at heart. They will know this about you; we give ourselves away with our smallest actions. To become a person of power, you must play true to your word.

A famous writer had long held a family secret regarding the cause of her mother's death. She lived in terror every time she published a book that some reporter would "out" her family, even though all the members were now adults and had made peace one way or another with their past. Finally, this writer openly explained the story to one of the more thoughtful journalists she met on a recent publicity campaign. This reporter did use the story, but with respect and sympathy, avoiding the vicious outing she had always lived in fear of.

Truth is the most powerful weapon because people are too weak to resist it. Speak the truth at first and no one can hurt you. A lawyer who tells the opposition everything they want to know about her client invariably ends up winning her cases. "Half the time they don't believe me anyway," she says. "That totally confuses them, and they don't know what to believe. They can't figure out whether I'm a simpleton or a genius. So I walk into the courtroom knowing what I know. They walk in not even sure of what they know."

Twelve
Enhance your strengths—stand tall

Understand what lies behind the antagonism on your opponent's part. What does he deeply care about? Most likely he cares more about his own success than about his challenge to you. This is so no matter what the war, or the struggle. Anger needs stoking in order to retain its heat. Few people have that sustained fire.

Most people don't really want to fight at all. They want to win. The most confrontational among us are usually scared, seeking to control everything they can. If you are someone's target, chances are he is more frightened of something that you represent—perhaps a power or an ability—than of you yourself. In school we called these people bullies.

Become the very image, the total embodiment, of the opponent your enemy fears. Your boss is afraid of your femininity. Your challenge, then, is to appear ultrafeminine and totally professional in behavior. A colleague is threatened by your creativity. Share an idea with her. Your spouse has been distant and withdrawn. Don't withdraw your affection in kind; lavish him with it.

Hannah Arendt, the political philosopher who escaped from Nazi Germany, said she fought the Nazis not in the guise of a "world citizen" who was calm, detached, and objective about the horrors. Rather, she fought them "as a Jew"—as the very embodiment of the intense, scholarly, introspective creature they feared. "When one is attacked as a Jew, one must defend oneself *as a Jew*," she wrote. According to her biographer, Elisabeth Young-Bruehl, "It motivated the positive outcome of her life in Berlin in 1933 when she transformed her personal problems"—criticism not for her ideas but for who she was, betrayal by old friends and mentors—"into an unambiguous political stance." *Act passionately but think straight* was her pattern. Arendt later became a Fury who pilloried the entire Nazi enterprise with one unforgettable and unparalleled phrase—"the banality of evil."

To act a role deliberately can shock the most complacent or intransigent opponent and most certainly will throw any antagonist into uncertainty. You suddenly live up to the picture others have of you. You offer them a self-caricature *and it is as though they cannot live with their own reality flung back at them.* They start to accept what just before they claimed to hate. It is *as if* they had created you and suddenly they must love what they created.

Thirteen
Train your inner voice to "hold its breath" for a while

Don't rush into action. Slow things down. Take command when you are ready and when the action is hottest.

Few could resist photographer Diane Arbus. She persuaded 1970s feminist fury Ti-Grace Atkinson to pose nude for the cover of *Newsweek*, she charmed albino sword swallowers into admitting their fears of knives, and she gained access to people and places no photographer had dared pursue. A woman friend still remembers the touch of her hand years after her death. Diane was very tactical. One of her lovers, Alex, remembered the first moment he saw her. " 'I noticed Diane moving in the background—weaving in and out among the other students . . . I fell in love. She was the first great love of my life.' The following day Alex asked Diane to take a walk with him . . . 'I told her, "I noticed you last night," and she said, "I know you did—it was all very much for you." She was completely aware . . . She had that instantaneous intuition coupled with *a cherishing slowness of response*. She always knew what was up, but she took her time about reacting.' "

Holding your breath as the world gasps and races onward gives you the chance to increase your understanding of a situation. It gives you an aspect of power: a woman who can slow down the hulking beast of events is nothing if not powerful.

Pausing gives you the advantage of rest and preparation and renewed action. It forces the enemy to act: he puts his own strategy out for inspection; he might even act to do the very work you wanted done. Few people can tolerate silence or stillness, and will show their hand rather than wait and watch.

Fourteen
Appeal to your enemies' "better selves"

Demonstrate perfect trust in your opponent.

Never exploit any sudden appearance of weakness or vulnerability on the part of your opponent. In fact, make him strong. Fill his spirit with poetry, acts of courage, story, song, possibility, as Sojourner Truth did when she confronted a hostile mob (see pages 143–44). Express your faith that your opponent doesn't want to hurt you or anyone. Explain how he will not lose anything by helping you or joining with you; he will in fact gain more. Your mood must be one of giving the opponent the courage to change. Most people want to do good. They love rewards. They need only to be reminded of their own best instincts and sense of fair play to act in accord with your wishes.

Fifteen
Rely on yourself for both your suffering and your triumph

Accept no outside support in your war—only the support of insiders. Don't go to your enemy's enemies. Don't try to curry their favor and set them against the person you identify as your opposition. You must keep the battle focused on your agenda, and yours alone.

If Gandhi had accepted the support of the United States in his confrontation with the British overlords, he would have ruined his chances at a clean win. The issues he fought to keep focused would have become muddied. His battle for freedom would have shifted into a contest between British and American imperialism. His agenda would have come in second.

Sixteen
Be ready to accept changes in the opponent and to readjust both your strategy and the goals of your campaign

Be continuously willing to persuade others, even as you remain ready to be persuaded yourself. Don't insist on anything. Don't argue on principle. Be guided by what, under changing conditions, feels true to you. Be firm and flexible.

If you are fighting for a raise in your salary or a rise in your lover's estimation, stay attuned to the boss's (or your lover's) feelings. Don't become blind to them. Stay so attuned that you are ready to help if he needs help. Remain, in principle, law-abiding. Meet your deadlines; obey the basis of the relationship you've established. *This is so that when you do flaunt one of the laws you had agreed upon, the situation of your revolt is chosen by you and is well defined. Only in that way does it become a statement to the opposition.* Gandhi demanded imprisonment. Magda did not oppose her husband's arrest. A princessa circumventing the demands of her job, or her promise to her lover, does it only once, as a declaration of war. Within these limits, you must accept and even demand those penalties that by your chosen action you have willingly invoked against yourself.

Understand that you will never achieve a great right without a great risk. When American colonists, led by Samuel Adams, refused to pay the tea tax to the British Parliament and—disguising themselves as Indians and boarding the ships on the night of December 16, 1773—threw the tea into Boston harbor, they helped bring on revolution.

"Preach against false doctrines," wrote George Eliot, and "you disturb feeble minds and send them adrift on a sea of doubt." Antigone's great gift was her willingness to dare to be right. Her great failure, which resulted in her death for her principles, was that she could not dare to be wrong, to hem in her own powers, to readjust her campaign.

Let your own wrongs change you. Know when to persuade and enlighten even as you remain ready to be persuaded and enlightened.

Seventeen

*Invite any suffering, even loss or humiliation,
rather than show that your ego is more
important than your goal*

If your opponent knows he can merely humiliate you
but not destroy you, then he has no power over you.
He will stop trying to hurt you.

Don't be deterred by small upsets. Define the battle
in terms of a long-range war, not isolated skirmishes.
No one episode is a defeat if you define your goal as
large.

Express to your opponent your faith in his inability
to persist in harming you. Ultimately, the enemy will
side with you, if for no other reason than you've
shown him you will win, and that in your winning, he
may acquire a greater reward or grander identity—his
own share of the power.

*Anger against the adversary and anger against the self
are inseparable. Deception of the opponent and deception
of the self are one and the same.*

The point of these tactics is that of a "double conversion," to use the words of psychologist Erik Erikson. You take the angry, hurtful, greedy, uncoopera-
tive, antagonistic person and "by containing his
egotistic hate and by learning to love" him *for* his flaws
(with his flaws, not in spite of them), you confront
him by enveloping him. You force him to regain his
hidden capacity to trust and to love. Your emphasis is

not on conquering but on curing "an unbearable inner contradiction." The first conversion is in containing your opponent's anger. The second is in overcoming your opponent's inner contradiction.

Every enemy is someone at war with himself. You just happen to get in the way. You yourself fight the inner enemy all the time, mistaking it for someone outside you, like a lover, mother, child, boss. Disarming an antagonist of his anger is a power stronger than all arms.

IV

The Ultimate Freedom Is Ending the Battle

NOTHING IS HARDER THAN END-ings. Up to this point, war has been presented as a game of fierce give-and-take and steely possibility. Here is the last tactic—for the art of unbuilding, of tearing down, of ending the battle.

Eighteen
The last power is the power of good-bye

If you've tried everything and an opponent remains an adversary, walk away. Be ready to withdraw. It is the only way you can keep your spiritual initiative for another day.

There is a Buddhist saying: "You must close the book." In their temples the statue of Wisdom, a woman, carries two objects: a book and a knife. They are her tools: a book for genius, and a knife to cut things off. The better part of wisdom lies in cutting things off, knowing what to end, and when and how to end it. The way you close the book, make the cut, affects whether there will be a continuing story.

Endings are of two kinds: good destruction and bad. Bad destruction is self-destruction. It means destroying something prematurely, before its time.

Bad destruction is not always plain to the eye. There was a woman, famous in some circles, who climbed mountains all over the world. She soloed many climbs. She trekked into China before it was opened up to outsiders. A few years ago she was leading a group through the Rockies when she went on ahead to test the trail. She noticed the drizzle of stones overhead, but kept going. The next minute, an avalanche broke loose and buried her instantly. She was the only one of her group to die.

She was remembered as brave, a woman who loved life. But was she? This woman had been walking to her death for forty years, always pushing herself beyond where it was useful to go. She wasn't brave at all. She was frightened and ultimately more at home with useless destruction than with its opposite. She could never say, "No, I'm scared, I'm unsure, let's go back." She sought out immense danger because only in those moments could she hide her fears, not eradicate them.

Intimacy terrified her because it left her no place to hide.

When a person ends her life, or ends a relationship without giving it the chance to ripen—that is self-destruction. When you leave a job for the wrong reasons—perhaps out of frustration or humiliation, not because you've come to the end of your usefulness—that is self-destruction. Tearing up a poem you've written instead of revising it, hurting a person with a blameful remark—these are endings without the possibility of a continuing story. Through these acts, you destroy something in yourself, perhaps the ability to enter into lasting ties.

The power of good-bye does not rest in bad destruction, but in good destruction.

Good destruction is the clean ending, the kind that brings resolution and closure. Knowing when to let go of a lover who doesn't honor you; ending a working relationship with a subordinate whom you are making too much of an effort to keep; terminating with a therapist who doesn't seem to hear you—these are good endings. And with them come new beginnings.

A princessa has to destroy the half-dead things in her life the way a forest fire destroys the barren ground, prepares it for new growth. Make a clear, clean end. Do not equivocate about walking away after you have thoroughly apprehended the situation.

Saying "No, it's over" opens your eyes to new possibilities. "No is the widest word we consign to Language," wrote poet Emily Dickinson. When she was forty-seven years old, she caught the eye of a widower, Judge Lord, who wanted to marry her, the "recluse of Amherst." Here was what seemed her first chance at love since she was spurned by Charles Wadsworth fifteen years earlier. Yet she said no. Was it her retreat to a safe, chaste position, or had she no feeling for Lord? When you walk away or turn your back on something or someone, you give yourself a strength that is poorly understood in this culture of gratification. You strengthen yourself to come back and fight again for what you truly desire, because the "no" builds your strength. A sense of possibilities grows and so does your determination to realize them when you are prepared to walk away.

What truly sets princessas apart may be exactly this: that they say no not to others but to themselves more often (and on bigger matters) than other women. Being strong about saying no to themselves means that every yes is real. George Eliot said the most outrageous good-byes; as outrageous as others were in their demands, she was in her refusals. In her lifetime, she turned her back on her father's strict rules of churchgoing, which branded her as unmarriageable. She fell in love with a married man and lived with him, exiling her even from her worldly literary friends. She said good-bye to the fashionable style of writing in Victorian sentimentalities, and clung to the ideal of writing only what was true, even if by the standards of her day it was criticized as crude. And then, when her lifelong "husband," George

Lewes, died, she refused to go to his funeral, broke down entirely—"her screams heard through the house"—and two years later married a man twenty years younger.

Princessas are never lured strictly by plans for a glorious new life. They realize that creation comes out of clean endings. Princessas understand that acknowledging limits may create greater freedoms. And there is no greater power than the freedom to walk away.

THE BOOK OF

Subtle Weapons

❧

"How do you know if you're going to die?" poet Naomi Shihab Nye remembers asking her mother. She answered, "When you can no longer make a fist."

I

How the Right Weapons Turn the War in Your Favor

✦ KNOWING WHAT YOUR WEAPONS are and how to use them is the final lesson in the princessa's education in war. Like conventional weapons—a sword, a fist—subtle weapons quickly change the power equation. They give you immediate strength, make enemies back off, move you closer to your desires. They are not the weapons typically used against you, like cutting humor, lies, anger, demands, guilt. Your weapons are the qualities, traits, accoutrements a woman relegates to the art of seduction, and fails to employ in the wars of success. On the physical side, your weapons are your clothes, voice, hair, jewelry, posture, makeup, and tears.

They work at full force when you know your story.

"The girl has no idea what she means," the crowd mocked the young martyr Ursula as she was put to death for refusing to become the concubine of Attila the Hun. That sentence has great resonance for the princessa; she knows what she means. Every woman tells a story about herself through her visible expressions of self. But *the princessa knows the story she conveys to others, and this is her strength.*

A fighter labors like the July sun to tell his or her story in terms few can ignore. Rocky Marciano was a great fighter who became an all-time champion by building strength, by shaping strategy, and then by understanding *what he meant* in terms of his strength. Before a fight, he completely envisioned his opponent before him when he worked out, before his punching bag, in bed beside him. During the last week, he took his mental training a step further by breaking his code of familiarity with himself, becoming an intimate stranger to himself in an effort to achieve monastic-like concentration.

Each successive day closer to the fight, he drew further in upon himself: he stopped reading mail and taking phone calls; stopped eating unfamiliar foods; refused any physical contact with others. By the night before the fight, he had effectively shut out everything but the fight itself. He thought about only his arms and legs and speed and endurance. *He concentrated on his strength—he became a bullet* of a man. He knew what he meant in the most intricate detail.

The equivalent for the princessa is knowing what story

she tells about her life—the things that speak for her. When she concentrates on them, when she learns what they mean, these ordinary things of her life become her weapons. This concentration on who you are, down to your ordinary details, makes you a weapon. You graduate from considering any aspect of yourself as decorative; there is no element of your strength that you have not become aware of, nothing about yourself you feel ashamed of.

In ancient Egypt both the pharaohs and their wives used exquisite hair styling, makeup, and a show of jewels to convey power. Today, women have access to them uniquely and use them. A princessa no longer relegates them to decoration or afterthought. She doesn't use her weapons to hide a mark or tame her hair into the latest style. She understands their meaning and uses it. She uses these things to convey the essential story of her life. *In front of a mirror in her mind's eye, she is Rocky.*

She starts with the story her life tells about her. The princessa should determine the defining moment in her life. This is the crux of her story. It defines her strongest image. Is she her father's daughter through and through, carrying out his work in the world? Is she a motherlike figure, a pietà, here to be tested for her strength and persistence, like Golda Meir, of whom an African minister said about his implicit trust in her, "You are like a mother to us." A princessa does not spurn that image or figure of herself. She uses it; she arms herself in it.

Is she a sorceress who must turn dust into diamonds, and make the impossible possible? What is the key to her character? This becomes the myth of herself around which she must gather and build her symbols to make herself unforgettable. For the princessa to establish herself as an archetypal figure sets her course—for herself and her opponents.

Princessas use that defining moment or characteristic to give meaning to their accomplishments. Is she a daddy's girl who breaks through by taking a stand for freedom, by redressing wrongs and using the spark of grief to build something new. Daddy's girls are modern-day Joan of Arcs. They do not seduce; they are dead serious about everything. Joan wanted to free her fatherland, her beloved France, from English tyranny. Much like her, in another country, Russia, in another time—the 1920s—Ayn Rand watched helplessly as her father was destroyed by Communism and anti-Semitism. When the state closed down his pharmacy, he taught himself carpentry. The authorities encouraged him to work for a year building school desks and chairs, then took his work without paying him. Rand never forgot these experiences, so much so that every word she published in her adopted English was a love lyric to capitalism and freedom.

A princessa who realizes her role trains all her weapons on making herself a force to be reckoned with. Rand used everything: her body, her intellect, her look. *She became the image—the sight and sound—of her strengths.* How was it that such an average-looking woman could be thought hypnotically beautiful and compelling? How could she command Nathaniel Branden, younger than her by twenty-five years, not only to love her ideas but to make love to her? He was seduced because she had the power of knowing what she meant. Nothing about her was extraneous or purposeless. Everything fed into her story of who she was; just as Rocky Marciano went to extremes each succeeding day before the fight, to know himself—bone, muscle, fiber—and deleted everything that was extraneous, even a phone call from a friend. This made Rand hypnotic. Her body may not have been as beautiful as Branden's twenty-six-year-old wife's; but he favored Ayn. She had learned how to convey her power. A weapon, no less than her strategy, is a means by which a princessa expresses her power.

What the princessa means is best conveyed by nonverbal symbols. Women rely heavily on communication and silence as their traditional weapons. But these lack the power of nonverbal symbols. Words can be ignored, misconstrued, doubted, or invalidated. People have natural, rational resistances both to words and silence. But a nonverbal symbol evades all such filters and scores a direct hit past the brain's standard defenses.

I once watched J., a princessa and a CEO, enter a meeting wearing a wide-brimmed hat and dark sunglasses, as if the world were her desert and she had to shield herself against its bleaching sun. Her costume was stark but attention-getting by virtue of its extremes. With it, she played the tension in the room brilliantly. She was visually dominant, but through the symbols of her hiddenness—the long black dress, the hat, the glasses. She quickly took command of the action.

When a photo of her baby was brought out, someone asked whom the baby resembled. J. pulled off the dark hat and specs. At first, her paleness under all that black was shocking and seemed quite vulnerable. Then it was transformed into something powerful. It was the tension between the two states, light and dark, fierce and tender, that focused the action and agenda on J. and made her even larger than life. Now, a year later, J. remains fixed in the minds of the people who attended that meeting. As with Cordelia, it doesn't matter that she is offstage for most of the play—or how many events go on without her.

J. made brilliant use of tension in the room using nothing but the symbols she wore—her weapons. She outfitted herself in these trappings as a soldier of fortune wears his khakis, or a politician his blue suit: they served to intensify her presence as formidable. They made her known and mysterious at the same time. Every person in the room disappeared in the shadow of her enormous—*but unaggressive*—presence. What she said became even more riveting because of the nonverbal symbols, and these focused on who she was.

There is a misperception that to be noticed in and of itself is a triumph. *How* you are noticed is a triumph of weaponry. An Armani suit and a great haircut display their wearer as decoration. You look like a

Class A object. But images that tell your story—whatever these images are—are weapons. Decorations are not weapons; they are the opposite. They make you weak to the nonverbal mind; they help you blend in, powerless.

A princessa cannot afford to think of herself only as her ideas or her talent or her CV or a wallet for that one great suit. A princessa is a story. She is a story whether she wants to be or not—because she is a woman. People watch women as if reading them—they watch them more closely than they do men because they are more interesting.

Women have been the subject of so much objectification because of their intrinsic mystery. The strength of that mystery more than the strength of patriarchal control may be the reason women are in "decorative" positions. Some of the greatest figures of worship are female: the Virgin Mary, Mother Nature, earth goddesses, Madonna! People study women the way the devout read books—not so much to learn material as to surrender to a word or phrase that captures one's attention. That is how others perceive women, and *that is why nonverbal symbols become weapons.*

That is why men who are unafraid of their own feminine traits also take greater command of any stage.

Eyewitnesses say about Golda, Joan, and Ayn that no one else existed in their midst. They were vast powers; they used weapons few women would think to use today to secure their stature.

The bird has its beak, and the lion its claws. Each

uses its essential nature. Using weapons is not a terrorist act. Overusing them is. And not using them is
equally harmful. A strength you don't use turns destructive. Generosity unexpressed hardens into bitter-
ness. Intelligence denied loops into deviance.

Ordinary men and women use weapons all the
time, only they are the cheap weapons of cutting humor; disapproval; half-truths; money; position; demands as unrelenting as an avalanche. These are not
for the princessa. A princessa's weapons are basic to
her being.

II

Know Your Shame, Love Your Power

YOUR SHAME IS YOUR KEY WEAPON. A princessa's weapons are the parts of herself she has long concealed, and which she now *uncon*ceals. These are things she has learned to hide, tame, or be shamed by. In a world that is frightened of women's power, it is no surprise that a princessa's strengths lie in the qualities she has tried to distance herself from. And in the very things that cause her shame she finds her greatest source of energy and stamina. An enormous effort gets put into submerging those traits.

For instance, tears are thought to be a sign of weakness. Success manuals insist a woman never cry in public. We treat our tears with shame. Yet Greek heroes spent a good part of their time lamenting—"They wept alike for joy or grief, tears like spring rain." They wept because they had seen horrors; but mostly they wept because they could. They knew the power of expression. Mark Twain wrote that Joan of Arc could cry at the drop of a hat; a leader who is half her time in tears is a leader with whom people can be honest, unguarded.

A woman who is unafraid to cry, who shows her tears, strengthens her presence—to others and to herself. Precisely because tears are a powerful weapon, the "message" is to keep them in check. One princessa battled her business manager to approve an expense she believed was necessary. The manager refused. His explanation was that she didn't need what she said she needed. So she met with him.

She laid out her arguments. He countered each one with the vaguest of explanations. She had a sense that he would let her argue until she gave up in exhaustion. She would feel she'd been listened to and would go away happy. The thought of this infuriated her. She was not just anyone asking for something special. She *was* special—she was responsible and had proven her success—and, yes, she was asking for something special that she believed she needed to do the work she wanted to do. Her business manager was treating her as just another problem. So she cried. As the tears drizzled down her cheeks, the business manager sat bolt upright in his chair, as if electrified, and sputtered, "If it means that much to you, I'll sign it." The meeting was over in thirty seconds.

A princessa uses tears for this reason: If you treat yourself as special, others will match your desire and sense of self by their own actions. They will mirror you. In other circumstances, tears could seem small and manipulative. But a princessa is playing to win a war, battle by battle. She realizes that the more she gets, the richer she is and the more generous she will be in turn. Operate from a position of scarcity, in a world where refusals are commonplace in your mind and experience, and you meter everything you give. *Operate from a position where you have what you want and your generosity isn't sacrificial, it's effortless.*

Tears are a freedom of speech issue. Most women rely on tears out of submission, and they are embarrassed when they use them. Princessas use them because they play beyond the rules; and nothing changes the game faster than tears.

A woman's breasts are another source of hidden power. The most famous warriors who made use of their body as a weapon were the Amazons, who fought with a breast exposed. The sight of a female nipple could stop an attacker in his tracks. This is not to say that the modern warrior should show cleavage. It is to say that a feminine presence wrapped in feminine clothes is a weapon. Much more so than the masculine costume we favor in today's workplace.

Breasting the waters is how swimmers take a strong current. Turn your chest toward a problem. Stand straight. Your breasts send a powerful message of femininity into the fray, and you stand a good chance of prevailing, as several social protesters in India discovered in 1971. A group consisting of men and women rounded a corner and found itself facing a crowd that was large, determined, and intent on confrontation. Its members advanced, brandishing knives and steel rods. The protesters braced for attack.

Then suddenly the women in the group stepped out and surrounded the men. Their hair, their skirts, became a thin, fluttering barrier, a wall. They turned to face the approaching hostile men, challenging them, daring them to attack by doing nothing more than turning their attention and their female forms on them. The thugs took a few more steps forward, then faltered, and ultimately retreated.

Another princessa, who plies her successful trade as a top media analyst, wears a necklace of five amulets: everything from a Maltese cross to a mystical Jewish hand to a pendant with the first line of Genesis engraved on it in French. She is understated about everything but the necklace. It is her signature. When people ask—and they always ask—she tells a story about each charm and what it means and why she wears it. You suspect that she has faced down a huge random catastrophe and survived it, and the charms are meant to ward off another date with destiny. Even if you don't consciously think this, there is a whiff of heroism in these charms, and a large fate attached to their wearer. But no matter what your guess, something else happens with these charms and her stories about them. She has made herself the focal point. Her stories put her in charge of the agenda. Others will now look to her. She has created a situation in which she doesn't insist on being heard; she *is* heard. Katherine Anne Porter bought herself the biggest emerald her money could buy after her novel, *Ship of Fools*, became a bestseller. Her young male admirers couldn't shake her hand without being nearly crippled by her success.

Jewels talk. They express a truth that goes deeper than words. Diderot tells the fable of a sultan who desires to know women's secrets. The sultan acquires a magic amulet. When he points it at a woman, her own jewel—"the sincerest part of her"—speaks the truth. In Diderot's story, the vagina is her jewel (a pun in French on *bijou*, which means both). The sincerest part of a woman is her sex; to give this "voice" is to conquer.

Few enemies and few lies can stand in the presence of a woman who expresses her unedited femininity. When the "jewels" speak in Diderot's story, men who have puffed themselves up with grandiose tales of their strength and prowess are revealed to be weak and the women, direct and honest, are the heroes.

Likewise, colors are like pheromones, the chemical agents known to induce feelings of love. They are powerful attractors. White is powerful because it disarms an opponent.

Gandhi wore white. Joan of Arc wore white. It marked her as a bull's-eye in battle, and therefore as fearless, invincible, above it all, above the fight. Look invincible and others are reluctant to take you on. White is the color of possibility. Paper is white; blank canvases are white. Wear white to a meeting and you break an opponent free from his tough stand or insistence on his own agenda. Negativity and refusal cannot stand in its presence. White signals that you are open to every possibility. It implies that problems or obstacles cannot exist in your presence. A princessa tells me that on two occasions when she wore an all-white suit, two powerful men fell in love with her. Such things happen all the time in the presence of white.

Vivid colors trigger much the same reaction: cobalt blue, not turquoise; red, not cranberry; yellow, not mustard. The standard colors women wear—gray, beige, pastels—are camouflage colors; they telegraph fear and uncertainty on the wearer's part, and therefore stimulate aggression on the opponent's. When a figure of power thinks you are weak, he despises you and does what he can to eliminate you.

In a culture of made-up women, sometimes the most powerful of all is an unadorned face. Eleanor Roosevelt wore her bare face the way a soldier wears his scars. Her face was her true medal. When she was thirty-four her life changed when she discovered her husband Franklin's shocking infidelity with her own trusted social secretary. It was a double betrayal. The suffering Eleanor experienced was total. In the aftermath, she drove miles out of Washington and spent several days each week at Rock Creek Cemetery before a statue of Clover Adams, wife of Henry Adams, the late-nineteenth-century philosopher and writer.

Clover, a photographer in the early days of the art, discovered Henry's love for another woman, and in despair she killed herself by drinking photographic acid. Her husband commissioned the statue to be erected in her memory. It came to be known as *Grief*.

That year, Eleanor could barely eat, and when she did, she could not always keep her food down. As a result, her teeth loosened, spread, protruded. Her grief etched itself on her face for the rest of her life, yet it became her pride, the medal for a contest she'd won. Even when they didn't know the facts, it was obvious to onlookers that something must have happened to take that face beyond ordinary plainness. It was a mythic portrait of sadness. No one of Eleanor's social and political status had to look so brutalized unless she chose to. But Eleanor used her appearance as a shield of strength, a weapon. Faces, Rebecca West says, are Marthas, referring to the biblical woman who was heaped with cares; faces say it all about one's character because of their close connection with the mind.

Finally, a princessa's voice is her prime weapon. It is a multifaceted instrument; pitch and volume are only part of it. Her voice is also the particular style of language she uses to communicate—more than the words themselves.

Concentrate on the sound and the forms of speech, even more than the message. Sojourner Truth, the slave who had bought her own freedom at the end of the Civil War, learned this under fire. On her way to give a lecture one night, she was confronted by an angry mob. She could run and hide, or try to reason with them. If she ran, her show of fear would only incite their hatred and make their attack more vicious. If she confronted them with one of her reasoned speeches, she would be speaking a foreign language. Reason did not equip them with sticks and knives, after all.

So she did the outrageous. She walked in full view of the mob and began to sing at the top of her voice. The men were shocked. They had no mob training in defending themselves against a song. They stopped, and listened. And as they listened, they softened. As they softened, they became persuaded by what she had to say. "Sing more, sister," they begged her. "Tell us about your life."

A princessa builds strength and authority into her voice in several ways:

- *She might talk louder than usual. To talk louder is to think louder.* It is difficult to say things you half-heartedly believe when you can hear yourself speak, and when you are sure others hear you clearly.
- *She uses declarations as a frequent weapon.* These are grenades of effectiveness. A declaration is a promise to yourself, a self-command: "I declare that I will never let my boss humiliate me again." A statement like that exerts a hypnotic pull on the speaker. What a princessa promises, she is more likely to do than anything she utters in any other form to her-

self. Resolutions do not have the power of declarations. Commitments of any other kind pale in power. A statement like "I don't want my boss to humiliate me again" does nothing for the princessa. Speak in declarations—which is tantamount to living by them—and *others will take you seriously because they know you mean what you say*. A positive declaration is more powerful than one expressed in the negative: "I will become a force in my business in the next ten months" implies that your boss will no longer be in a position to humiliate you.

- *Commands* are rarely used by women, but used early in a relationship, they *establish your strength*. Wu Yi, a tough fighter and China's trade minister, commanded her opposite on the U.S. side to "sit" the first time she met her. Startled, the U.S. negotiator promptly obeyed. From then on, the Americans felt uncertain in Wu Yi's presence. She got the edge from the start.

- *A princessa who is verbally attacked never reacts to another's attack. She never responds directly.* That would put her in the position of fighting her enemy's war, always a losing battle. A venture capitalist called a meeting to update everyone on a new deal. Her partner had a different agenda. Before everyone was seated, she began by hijacking the meeting. "When is this program going to be ready?" she demanded. That was the purpose of the meeting, but she let no one offer an answer while she continued her rapid-fire attacks. "We have targets for tight delivery dates, and I see no assurance you'll make them." Her partner in the deal replied, "We have programs to address these problems." "My commitments are on the line," her antagonist shot back. "But we're prepared to meet them." "There are no penalties here for not meeting them." On it went, the hijacker caring more about establishing her superiority in order to win maximum concessions, and her partner taking her bait again and again, reacting to these attacks, sounding like a machine gun as she spewed out her but-but-buts. Finally, she realized what was happening and switched to offense. "Okay," she said. "If you don't trust my ability to deliver, you're free to pull out of this deal. Do it right now." That was it. The aggressor shut up and everyone moved on to the agenda.

III

On the Use of Men as Weapons

A PRINCESSA'S SUCCESS DOES not depend on eliminating men from her life or surrounding herself with weak men. Women have often felt that men are the enemy. "Men are useless," a woman of fierce independence publicly contended. To say that men are useless is to say that great works of art are also useless. As women have begun to taste power, those who get further have been able to make peace with men. To do so makes use of men as allies.

There are two avenues for achieving an alliance with men in which your power is not compromised: through disempowerment and through friendly rivalry.

As much as women crave empowerment, men

crave disempowerment—they actually want to risk giving up some of their control. They are not willing to do this with another man, but they are with a woman. If a woman clearly takes charge, knows her mind, her story, a man will gratefully lay down his burden of power at her feet, and sigh like Atlas taking the world off his aching shoulders.

This is best understood by recognizing the fundamental conflict between men and women. It is this: men are afraid of women. Some men welcome that fear to keep them sharp.

A princessa recognizes that this fear and women's sorrow over it can never be changed or cured. So she uses it. She helps it surface by her behavior. Once that fear is evident, she tries to convert its energy into power for both parties.

A princessa notices that in a meeting the seat next to a powerful figure is often left vacant. She takes that seat, not contact-close, but close enough to throw him off his game, make him stretch out of routine ways of talking and behaving and thinking. Remember Inanna. A princessa does not believe in trying to comfort a man at the cost of reducing her power. She lets him know that she sees inside him, past his expensive shoes and tailored suit.

When a princessa met a multimillionaire owner of a major sports franchise, who bosses around players the size of Brahma bulls, he was thrown when she sat next to him. His foot started waving like a metronome, his hands became part of his talk, as if thrown up in self-defense. All she did was sit beside him on the sofa and look straight at him as he spoke. She used the weapon of her body in close proximity only to disarm him—to wake him up in ways that other men, predictable blank slates for him, couldn't. Her closeness played against the tension of her totally professional and sharply intelligent manner. Nothing here was a come-on. Just the opposite. But he would remember her favorably as someone powerful enough to sit beside him as an equal as the other men in the room rushed to the sidelines for cover, respectful but cowed.

As a friendly rival, a princessa realizes that playing off a man's strengths gets them both noticed. Jackie Onassis is remembered today because of the men in her life. Would Simone de Beauvoir be as highly thought of if she hadn't been paired with Jean-Paul Sartre? Or Eleanor with Franklin? Or Hillary with Bill Clinton? This is still a man's world, and any friendly rivalry you can induce will become a powerful weapon in the service of your abilities.

Remember: *Ask for everything.* This is highly effective in any situation. A negotiator tries to find common ground and expects each side to compromise. A princessa shifts the other's ground so that her agenda prevails. The opposing side knows it's lost something, but what it gains is greater. Thus a good negotiator will always make a task seem possible and let the opponent know he is halfway there. *But a princessa will always make a task seem larger than possible, to draw on people's heroic instincts and strengths.* She knows people rise more readily to larger tasks than to smaller ones; and she enlarges the task by asking for everything, and enlarges their strength at the same time.

Don't fear "no"s. Give people the chance to say "no" to you. If they say it enough, they will feel beholden to you to come back with a "yes" by way of compensation.

Ask for everything because nothing less is worth having. People are more giving if your request challenges them to be heroic. Asking for small things makes both asker and asked feel small. People are drawn to big ideas and big adventures more passionately than to small ones.

Golda Meir would ask for everything by talking up Israel's problems as her problems. When she tried to raise money and support for Israel's War of Independence, she kept her stories of need and desire intimate, talking of conversations with specific soldiers, not in terms of abstract "troops" or "numbers" or political ideologies. Listeners caught up in your story won't turn you away. It becomes their problem too. "You win a war," Golda said, "by making it everyone's, not yours alone."

Melanie Klein drafted the formidable Dr. Freud as her strong if unwitting ally to build the base of her power. No one weaker would do as her helpmate. In her early years Klein had been his student and his devotee. Then she realized she would get further as his collaborative enemy.

She did something more ingenious than split with his philosophy. She built a familial antagonism between herself and Freud's daughter Anna. She began to oppose their ideas and honor his brilliance—her use of strategic tension. This brought others in her profession to a fever pitch. Some defended Freud, some her. The battle lines were drawn. Her colleagues could not turn her out of the psychoanalytic movement. Instead, they engendered her opposition with a storm of protest against her. The result was that Melanie Klein gained prominence throughout Europe, not only because of the controversy she generated but because of her ideas. Klein benefited from the controversy, and so did Freud. She elevated both of their ideas to international prominence.

Mary Lindell, a British spy whose dangerous work in the World War II underground saved hundreds of Allied soldiers from death at her own daily risk, was eventually captured. Taken into custody, she was asked by her Nazi guard, "How come a smart woman like you got caught?" She said, "I've noticed that a foolish woman can control a smart man. She can manipulate him into buying her clothes, dinners, anything." Then she looked her enemy square in the eye. "But while a foolish woman can control a smart man, it takes a very smart woman to control a fool." Mary Lindell could not be stopped, except eventually by old age. Captured, tried by a Nazi court, she was jailed in solitary confinement, sent to a concentration camp, released, shot, beaten—and survived all these horrors.

An enemy is a fool, and a princessa must be smart—cognizant—about her weapons, her strategy. She must leave nothing to ignorance and her own unawareness.

IV

The Polish Generalissimas' Paradigm

THE "OTHER WOMAN" IS AN AR-chetype of fear—except in war, where she is the best weapon loyalty can buy.

Women sabotage women, goes the common belief. It's one of the reasons women never think of other women as weapons in their own fight. As friends, yes; as counselors, yes. But in a fight, women typically never expect other women to help them; they expect them to steal a man, subvert praise, or just ruin something valuable.

A woman highly placed in a major Silicon Valley company confessed that she goes out of her way to keep other women down. "There are maybe two vice presidency slots allotted to women managers in my company. Do you think I'm going to help another woman who could ace me out for that slot?" Science even has a female name for the eat-your-young, devour-your-own maneuver, the Red Queen Syndrome. It goes like this: A lion chasing a herd of deer needs to capture only one. As long as one deer is weak and slow, the others in the pack don't have to run that fast, especially if they can make sure the slowest lags behind accordingly. As long as women define their game as small and limited, women will fight each other or give each other up to satisfy the big predator.

But women won't do this to each other if they can engage in a bigger game of love and war.

In a change-the-game situation, women are powerful weapons to other women. Two women in the Polish revolutionary hierarchy made this idea legendary. They each realized they could get further faster if they boosted the career of the other. So when Tereza went off to a dinner party, she boasted of Agnes's successes, not her own husband's. When Agnes appeared at a meeting, she promoted Tereza for a job that came up. They became famous as "the Polish generalissimas' paradigm." Inside their circle, each woman, through dint of the other's repeated reminders, took on increased status. Their colleagues soon took up their refrain, telling one another, "I understand Tereza already tried that." Or, "Agnes made such a success of this problem . . ." Each got promoted to high positions at exactly the same time.

In the German concentration camps, women were

routinely organized by their guards into groups of five. The bonds developed by the "fivehoods" were one of the reasons women outnumbered male survivors throughout the camp system. They acted as mothers, sisters, daughters to each other, strengthening the will to survive. On their own, with no organized brotherhoods, the men suffered greater fatalities.

No story matches Erna Rubinstein's. When there was no food or water, when her mouth became dry and she couldn't produce any saliva to swallow, she became frantic. In these times, the oldest of her fivehood, her friend Anna, would hold on to her, but pretended that she, Anna, needed the holding. Anna also told Erna stories of her son in another camp. She described how brave and beautiful he was, and the dishes she used to cook for him, down to the last pinch of salt. Erna could smell the soup in her mind; it made her mouth water. The old woman said she had to save Erna because one day she would marry her son and be the mother of his children.

Everyone knew this was ridiculous. The woman's son had been killed; his clothes and papers had been returned to her, and kept in a box under her bunk. She insisted that the Nazis had given her these things to destroy her; her son was not dead. The old woman held on until the camps were liberated, then she died. Recovered from her trauma, Erna became a high official in postwar medical rehabilitation circles. Traveling to inspect a new hospital, she heard of a doctor in need of work. Erna met him, thought him qualified, and secured him a position in her hospital. They spent time together, fell in love, and married. At that point, he entrusted her with the details of his past. He told her how through stealth he had managed to escape certain death in the camps. He was sure his parents were dead, and as he described his mother to her, Erna realized that she had been the "mother" of her fivehood, the woman who had kept Erna alive for this meeting with fate.

When you act to remove false obstacles such as fear of another's success, as the Polish generalissimas did, or the concentration camp sisters had to do, you find the most effective weapons of all are the people in the very same boat as you.

EPILOGUE

Strategy for a Wild Peace

My heart is like a chinese vase; it cracks many
times, but it never breaks.
—Gypsy Rose Lee

PRINCESSA, I CANNOT LET YOU
end your study of war without having a glimpse
of peace. Otherwise, you will look for peace and mistake it for one of its fakes and forgeries. You will assume that peace is born out of a win, or a defeat. You
will confuse peace with its sister, quiet. You will believe it when the Buddha says you attain peace by
subtracting your desire, or calming your agitation.
Peace, sing the choirs, is the lion lying down beside the
lamb. Definitions like this nearly made me decide
peace was more trouble than war. Princessas live for
excitement, heat—can I do this, can I succeed at that?
They don't want to give up their lion nature; they are
bored lying down beside lambs!

Peace is something else for the princessa: it is tranquility, fearlessness, and freedom, all three together.

I didn't know this when I began researching stories of peace in the biographies of great women. I habitually flipped to the back of the book, to the end of the story, figuring that peace came when they realized there was nothing left to fight for.

I never found peace there. At the end of their stories, I found resignation.

In traditional stories, peace and calm and resignation come with death—with giving up the battle entirely, or the need for fighting. Medusa, beheaded by Perseus, falls to the shore. The looks that killed and the hair of snakes that made her a feared fighter come into contact with the peaceful water. At that moment, her hair turns into pink coral. The message is that when Medusa quiets down, she becomes an everlasting beauty. Lady Macbeth, another unstoppable fury, finds no peace in life; instead, she is resigned to sleepwalk her way to death.

Giving up, making a truce, finding a place for rest and comfort—these are not peace. In the princessas' lives, things are different. *Peace comes, now and again, in the middle of the action.* A princessa at peace is the eye of a storm. Her art lies in finding these moments and in sustaining them; she knows they won't last forever but will return.

Peace is not the absence of war. Peace is the moment between battles and is defined by them. It is not separate from war. *The peace that a princessa thrives under is a "wild peace."* It is the feeling in your heart after great excitement: the feeling of satiety, or certainty, when all the world's concerns drop away and beauty like a lazy white foam rises up to take their place. It is the effortlessness after the effort. Peace comes in the middle of the fray. Isadora Duncan whirling like a dervish onstage knew peace. At rest, offstage, she was always tormenting herself with the drive to be better, to attain another glory. But moving at full fever, she was at peace. Her wars brought her to the stage of France's great theater, where she won the chance to perform in her own style. Dian Fossey, in a state of excitement, lay down in the dirt of the blazing jungle, fire ants all around, and thrust out a hand to touch the ape she called Peanuts in the first human contact with a great ancestor. That is peace. It is an instant of fullness where you feel the value of what you have been fighting for. This is peace as a symptom of joy and as such is tranquility, fearlessness, and freedom.

Inside each of these moments—for Dian, for Isadora, for all princessas—is a hidden script in which a woman says what she does not want. Ballerina Suzanne Farrell fell in love with her teacher George Balanchine and made her decision not to sleep with him. She said, "Our unique relationship had proved itself . . . often to both of us, and it might not have withstood consummation. The physical side of love is of paramount importance to many people, but to us it wasn't. Our interaction was physical, but its expression was dance." The critic Roger Shattuck says that Farrell's point is the same one he had learned looking at a night star: "Don't look directly at it, look slightly to one side of it." Peace is not saying no to things; refusals lead only to comfort—which is a false peace. Peace is understanding what you don't want; it's looking slightly off the goal.

Peace does not mean you limit your desires; it requires a counterintuitive way of valuing your desires. Women, like junkies, bounce between extremes where desire is concerned. They fight like hell, or they disown their wins. In any case, they find little peace in success. The peace that yields the greatest possibilities is a wild peace. Because there are few stories of wild peace in princessas' histories, I have turned to the best story I know of peace in the heart of conflict. It is a soldier's story.

I was drawn to this soldier because of four words that still echo in my mind: "Epictetus, here I come." The soldier said these words as he ejected from his burning bomber into what was to become a ten-year saga of torture, deprivation, and punishment as a POW in North Vietnam. Why did he fall into Epictetus's arms, *as if he intended to do so*, as if he were making good on a promised rendezvous? "Epictetus, here I come" sounds like a date long postponed. These are eerie words from a fighter desperate to meet up with this chilling, missing part of his education which success never provided. Peace was Epictetus's expert subject.

The soldier had been free of captivity for close to a decade when he met me at the door of his office, then quickly sat down, cradling close to him that leg of his which had been cracked by his tormentors in more places than a Ming vase, holding it as the Virgin in the statue cradles her dying son in her lap. He could hear me when I shouted questions to him—like his captors, I thought—but he himself talked in whispers.

He took me back in time. He told me that in one minute he'd gone from an air wing commander cutting across the treetops, lining up to drop bombs on a railroad yard, to someone with no options. There he was, 10,000 feet above the earth, aiming for a target below, and just then a great big automatic gun that was not there the day before opened up and blew him out of the sky. His station in life instantly changed from the king of all he surveyed as an air wing commander to the lowest form of life in North Vietnam. From success to abject failure, I have the urge to say. But that is not the story at all. *He went from acquiring wins to a way of living in which winning was a natural state*—a state that resulted in tranquility, fearlessness, and freedom.

He did this, in a strange way, by transforming himself from a masculine state of being in control to a feminine state of having little control. Few men notice limits on their freedom in work, in thought, in what they can ask for. This soldier learned what it was like to be womanly—in a way, powerless.

At the moment of his capture, he was in control of

his destiny. He thought he had the certainty of love: he was married to a beautiful, devoted wife. He had loving children. He thought he had control of his station in life: he was much decorated, and on a career path that would lead to greater advancement. Now he controlled nothing.

The Epictetus he called out to had lived centuries earlier as a slave. As a slave, he taught himself how to be free, mentally and emotionally, though he was under the tight rein of his masters. He found an ultimate peace on earth. Epictetus's reflections became the favorites of men who had everything—every freedom, all the world's money and power—yet felt no peace with all their winnings. The emperor Marcus Aurelius memorized Epictetus's sayings. The name they go under is Stoicism. Stoics are flustered by nothing. Their sense of peace makes a deep disruption in their lives impossible. As a young officer, our hero had read Epictetus's writings, and loved their beauty and depth. But with all his training in warfare, he had never had the chance to practice Epictetus's wisdom, until now, until this rendezvous with fate.

Could he as a prisoner know about the pain of a single mother in the grip of a terrible job and no options; or a woman whose lover walks out leaving her the hostage of her fears of loneliness; or a parent who stares into the face of a mortally sick child; or a manager who gets everything—her promotion, her darling—and then wonders, "Is this all there is?" When this soldier learned peace, he learned it for these women.

This is Epictetus's strategy for peace. This was what our brave soldier found worthy to risk dying for. It is one of the simplest, most effective ways for achieving peace that keeps you in the action, not hermetically safe from the action:

1. *Learn the distinction between the things in your power and the things not in your power.*

"If you earnestly seek that which is not your own, you lose that which is your own," Epictetus wrote. If, in other words, you set your heart on your health, your love, your pleasure, your career, you'll regret it. None of these things are completely in your power. Define yourself in terms of them and you are the enemy's captive, whether you are in a POW camp or in the arms of the wrong person or in an environment presided over by a malevolent boss.

But you can't say to yourself, "Okay, these things mean nothing to me. I don't care about my lover's attitude toward me, my health, or the state of my finances. After all, I don't control these things." You can't dismiss the things you care about. You can't eliminate your desire for them, as the Buddhists advise. You have to create a different relationship to them.

2. *Want the things you care about, desire them, strategize to get them—but never take them seriously.*

Play at getting them, play hard, play as if the game were a war game. But then, after the war, after the strategizing, learn to treat these very things you want *indifferently*.

3. *To treat precious things indifferently, understand the nature of all games, even war games*.

The soldier draws an analogy to a tennis game. The whole afternoon may be devoted to this tennis ball. You aim the ball here, you aim it there. You are using that external thing, that ball. But after the game is over, does anybody give a damn about that ball? Not at all. It's left behind for one of the players to pick up and put in the bottom drawer. It means nothing to anybody that's spent the afternoon playing with it.

That is how to treat the things you value most—your health, your love, your prestigious job—indifferently. You play with them, fight for them—they are the tennis ball—but you *don't internalize any of them*. Don't count on any of them or you become their slave. Don't count on your lover's promise to always be with you. Don't expect your job to be there tomorrow. Fight for it, but be ready to put your idea of your perfect job in the bottom drawer and go on. Don't expect your poet's vision or any gift you have to be as compelling always as it is now.

"Your master," said Epictetus, "is he who controls that on which you have set your heart or wish to avoid."

4. *Ask yourself: Have I allowed myself to be trapped by any of these things? Have I fought for them, won them, and now mistake them as mine? If I have, my wins will bring me no peace or joy.*

The soldier explained how desires worked in prison camp: "The prison interrogator had as his number one job 'getting the prisoner on the hook,' getting him to set his heart on something that his captor controls. He says to me, 'Do you want water?' I don't say 'Yes!'; I don't say 'No!' I learned to say, 'It's up to you.' That's the way you can stay out of trouble, that's the way you stay out of entanglements. When you get good at this, you come to a point where no one can harm you without your permission."

Imagine what it means to treat water indifferently when it is given out teaspoon by teaspoon in the burning jungle, not when you crave it but seemingly at random. What is as vital as this water to the princessa? Her child's smile, her mother's approval, her boss's praise? She may be parched for these things, but she says to herself about each, "It is up to them. I do not control their responses. I cannot buy their favor. I can work like hell on this job, but if it's to get an A, I'll be disappointed. I can use the strategy, I can act according to the eighteen tactics, but though these will give me my best chance at winning, I cannot count on the outcomes I fully desire. The minute I think I can determine another's responses to ensure my win, that's the minute they have gotten me on the hook and I become their prisoner. Because if I say I won their favor, I must also be responsible for causing their disapproval. And if I think that, I am always their captive, never at peace, no matter how good my work or my actions."

5. *If you try to control that which is not your own, you lose that which is your own.*

Understand that you control nothing but your perceptions. Nothing can hurt you unless you give it the power to hurt you.

If you set your heart by your career, your pleasure, your happiness, you'll regret it. That which is your own is your view of a situation.

When your health stumbles, when your lover hurts you, when a boss talks to you the way no one on earth should address another, find your center. When you come back from a vacation to a message from your boss screaming "URGENT," you have a choice. You can drop everything, including your calm, and act in emergency-response mode. Or you can respond to this noxious command in your own fashion. When your mother leaves an "urgent" message for the eleventh day in a row, when she just wants attention, or when a client bursts in on you without an appointment, you can give them your driver's license along with the wheel, or you can determine who owns the road on this particular trip. As long as you're not taken in by "urgent" and are rather captivated by the overdone drama of "URGENT," your boss or mother or client cannot control you; they cannot undo the calm of your vacation or your equilibrium. And when they see they cannot hook you, not only are you free, but they stop trying to bait you.

"What are the tragedies but the portrayal in tragic verse of the sufferings of people who have admired things external," Epictetus said. Lear, who demanded ingratiating demonstrations of love; Lady Macbeth, who would share the Scottish throne with her husband and wouldn't stop until she got there—they wanted "things external." Tragic figures may get close to what they want—kingdoms, devotion, a shot at the top job—but they never get peace from their winnings.

6. *Peace Is Wild.*

Feel a wild peace. It is not calm. It's an imperative of the field like wild flowers, wrote Israeli poet Yehuda Amichai. I know it when I think of Dresden, a city flattened by bombs in World War II, which spent no time in agony or recrimination but set about immediately to rebuild itself out of the rubble. That is wild peace. I think of the American homefront during that war. The United States was marked by more "free love" in the 1940s than in the '60s. In the '40s, free love meant sacrificing butter and eggs and gas for the boys at the front. It meant all-night prayer vigils, and round-the-clock assembly lines, and greeting strangers as friends and friends as family. The world was at war, but the United States was marked by love and peace.

Peace comes in the thick of things, not as an aftermath. You won't taste peace unless you are in the heart of war, not apart from it.

Whether coming off a victory or a defeat or a truce, princessas are always running into Epictetus's arms, embraced by his words. Those are their truest rendezvous.

Ask yourself, when you are afraid or on the verge of a breakthrough: When does a candle shine the brightest?

The answer is always in the dark.

NOTES

Page xi Katherine Anne Porter, *The Collected Essays* (New York: Dell, 1973), p. 56.

Page xi The parable of the sisters adapted from James R. Mellow, *Charmed Circle: Gertrude Stein and Company* (New York: Avon Books, 1975), p. 59.

Page 4 Arbus quote from Patricia Bosworth, *Diane Arbus: A Biography* (New York: Norton, 1995), p. 303.

Page 6 Machiavelli quote from Sebastian de Grazia, *Machiavelli in Hell* (Princeton, N.J.: Princeton University Press, 1990), p. 266.

Page 7 Concept of tradition: Frederick Turner, from an unpublished essay on Miklós Radnóti, 1996.

Page 10 *collaborative antagonist:* Albert Murray, *The Hero and the Blues* (New York: Vintage Books, 1995), p. 37.

Pages 10–11 Roberta Reeder, *Anna Akhmatova: Poet and Prophet* (New York: St. Martin's Press, 1994).

Page 12 Irene Mahoney, *Madame Catherine* (New York: Collier Books, 1966).

Page 12 Anne Somerset, *Elizabeth I* (New York: St. Martin's Press, 1991), p. 94.

Page 13 Vita Sackville-West, *Saint Joan of Arc* (New York: Image Books/Doubleday, 1991).

Page 13 Mark Twain, *Personal Recollections of Joan of Arc* in *Historical Romances* (New York: Library of America, 1994).

Pages 13–14 Farley Mowat, *Woman in the Mists: The Story of Dian Fossey and the Mountain Gorillas of Africa* (New York: Warner Books, 1987).

Page 14 Ralph G. Martin, *Golda Meir: The Romantic Years* (New York: Charles Scribner's Sons, 1988).

Page 15 Octavio Paz, *Sor Juana: Or, The Traps of Faith* (Cambridge, Mass.: Belknap Press of Harvard University Press, 1988), p. 73.

Page 15 Sojourner Truth, *The Narrative of Sojourner Truth*, ed. Henry Louis Gates, Jr. (New York: Schomburg Library of Nineteenth Century Black Women Writers, 1991), p. 116.

Page 16 Story of boy and duck restaurant, recounted by Betty Sue Flowers at the Currency Shakespeare Seminar, June 1996, New York City.

Page 16 Isadora Duncan, *My Life* (New York: Liveright, 1927).

Pages 18–19 Benazir Bhutto, *Daughter of Destiny: An Autobiography* (New York: Simon & Schuster, 1990).

Page 19 Victoria Glendinning, *Rebecca West* (New York: Knopf, 1987).

Page 21 Erik H. Erikson, *Gandhi's Truth: On the Origins of Militant Nonviolence* (New York: Norton, 1970).

Page 21 James Baldwin, "The Fight: Patterson vs. Liston," *Antaeus* 62 (Spring 1989).

Pages 21–22 Tom Robbins, *Even Cowgirls Get the Blues* (New York: Bantam Books, 1977), p. 73.

Page 23 "The Book of Strategy" epigraph based on a line about war and knowledge from Carlos Castaneda, *Journey to Ixtlán: The Lessons of Don Juan* (New York: Washington Square Press, 1972), p. 267.

Page 25 Idea of the loftiness of spying from Roseanne: "I have always understood—by virtue of my own battlefield experience at home, during childhood—[that] the highest degree of ethics, consciousness, and gamesmanship attainable to women is actually 'spy.' " From an unpublished essay.

Page 31 Five Whys adapted from Peter Senge et al., *The Fifth Discipline Fieldbook* (New York: Currency/Doubleday, 1995), pp. 108–12.

Pages 33–34 Observations on the truth adapted from John Lahr, "Dealing with Roseanne," *The New Yorker*, July 17, 1995.

Page 37 Rebecca West, *Black Lamb and Grey Falcon: A Journey Through Yugoslavia* (New York: Penguin Books, 1994).

Page 38 Janet Wallach, *Desert Queen: The Extraordinary Life of Gertrude Bell* (New York: Doubleday, 1996).

Page 41 Akhmatova facts: Reeder, op. cit.

Pages 41–42 Marilyn Yalom, *Blood Sisters: The French Revolution in Women's Memory* (New York: Basic Books, 1994).

Page 42 Persephone: Edith Hamilton, *Mythology: Timeless Tales of Gods and Heroes* (New York: Mentor, 1969), p. 54.

Pages 42–43 Joan of Arc story: Mark Twain, op. cit.

Pages 44–46 Philosopher/teacher story derived from private conversation with an anonymous source.

Page 48 Quotation from John Evans from a private conversation.

Page 50 Quotation from *Howards End* cited in Adrienne Rich, *Of Woman Born: Motherhood as Experience and Institution* (New York: Norton, 1986), p. 66.

Page 51 Poet and critic Fred Turner, in numerous speeches, declaims on the social stature of poets.

Page 52 Alanis Morissette quote from "Better to Sing the Teen-Age Life than Live It," by Jon Pareles, *New York Times*, February 18, 1996.

Page 59 Quotation from Lou Andreas-Salomé cited in Lisa Appignanesi and John Forrester, *Freud's Women* (New York: Basic Books, 1992), p. 244.

Page 61 Catherine S. Manegold, "Tempering Troubled Waters: Myrlie Evers-Williams," *New York Times*, February 20, 1995.

Page 61 *Most people live in their dreams* . . . : from Castaneda, op. cit., p. 91.

Page 62 Bell story: Wallach, op. cit.

Pages 64–67 Magda Trocmé story from Philip Hallie, *Lest Innocent Blood Be Shed: The Story of the Village of Le Chambon and How Goodness Happened There* (New York: HarperCollins, 1994), p. 163.

Page 74 Four kinds of tension, used in different form and with different terms in Elaine Scarry, "War and the Social Contract: Nuclear Policy, Distribution, and the Right to Bear Arms," *University of Pennsylvania Law Review* 139, no. 5 (May 1991).

Page 80 *power anorexia:* the phrase was first used in a conversation with Betty Sue Flowers.

Pages 90–92 Diane Wolkstein and Samuel Noah Kramer, *Inanna: Queen of Heaven and Earth* (New York: Harper & Row, 1983).

Pages 92–93 Concubines story: Sun Tzu, *The Art of War*, trans. Samuel B. Griffith (London: Oxford University Press, 1963), pp. 57–58.

Pages 94–95 Fossey story: Mowat, op. cit.

Page 95 Gandhi story: Erikson, op. cit.

Pages 95–97 Connie Bruck, "Hillary the Pol," *The New Yorker*, May 30, 1994.

Page 98 Gandhi story: Erikson, op. cit.

Page 100 *Think through the body:* Scarry, op. cit., p. 1290.

Page 101 Gandhi and ahimsa: Erikson, op. cit.

Page 101 Phrases in Section Three derive from Gandhi's philosophy of nonviolence, as described by Erikson, op. cit.

Page 102 Tactics of the Zapatistas, reported in *The Economist*, special supplement on high-tech warfare, September 3, 1994.

Page 103 Phyllis Grosskurth, *Melanie Klein: Her World and Her Work* (Cambridge, Mass.: Harvard University Press, 1987), pp. 310–33.

Page 105 *Reduce the conflict to its bare essentials:* Erikson, op. cit.

Page 106 *Study every situation for its opposite:* Erikson, op. cit.

Page 108 *Be ready to get hurt and yet not inflict hurt:* Erikson, op. cit.

Page 108 *Be true* . . . . : Erikson, op. cit.

Page 108 *Never exact revenge:* Erikson, op. cit.

Page 109 On George Eliot's lack of beauty: Gordon Haight, *George Eliot: A Biography* (London: Penguin Books, 1992), pp. 115–16.

Page 109 On George Eliot's strategies: Ruby V. Redinger, *George Eliot: The Emergent Self* (New York: Knopf, 1975).

Page 110 *Let something new enter to destroy a boundary:* Erikson, op. cit.

Pages 110–11 Mellow comment about Stein: op. cit., pp. 27–28.

Page 111 *Conduct your campaign entirely in the open and at close range:* Erikson, op. cit.

Page 111 Mary Lindell quote from the film *One Against the Wind* (1991).

Pages 113–14 Elisabeth Young-Bruehl, *Hannah Arendt: For Love of the World* (New Haven: Yale University Press, 1982), p. 109.

Page 114 *Train your inner voice to "hold its breath" for a while:* Erikson, op. cit.

Page 114 Arbus story: Bosworth, op. cit., p. 296.

Page 116 *Appeal to your enemies' "better selves":* \Erikson, op. cit.

Page 116 Sojourner Truth, op. cit., p. 116–17.

Page 116 *Rely on yourself for both your suffering and your triumph:* Erikson, op. cit.

Page 117 *Be ready to accept changes in the opponent . . . :* Erikson, op. cit.

Page 118 Quote from George Eliot: Redinger, op. cit., p. 315.

Page 119 *Invite any suffering, even loss or humiliation . . .* : Erikson, op. cit.

Page 121 *The last power is the power of good-bye:* Erikson, op. cit.

Page 122 Buddhist saying, quoted in Deborah Kolb, "Negotiating Women," unpublished paper.

Page 122 Story of brave climber: recounted in private conversation by John Tarrant.

Pages 123–24 Roger Shattuck, "Emily Dickinson's Banquet of Abstemiousness," *New York Review of Books*, June 6, 1996.

Pages 124–25 George Eliot story: from Haight, op. cit., p. 516.

Page 127 Naomi Shihab Nye, *Words Under the Words: Selected Poems* (Portland, Oreg.: Eighth Mountain Press, 1995), p. 68.

Page 130 Ursula story: Kathleen Norris. *The Cloister Walk* (New York: Putnam, 1996), p. 138.

Page 130 Rocky Marciano facts: Joyce Carol Oates. *On Boxing* (Garden City, N.Y.: Doubleday/Dolphin, 1987), pp. 28–29.

Page 131 Peggy Mann, *Golda: The Life of Israel's Prime Minister* (New York: Washington Square Press, 1973), p. 172.

Pages 132–33 Rand's childhood: Claudia Roth Pierpont, "Twilight of the Goddess," *The New Yorker*, July 24, 1995.

Page 133 Barbara Branden, *The Passion of Ayn Rand* (Garden City, N.Y.: Doubleday, 1986).

Page 138 Quote about Greek heroes: Porter, op. cit., p. 137.

Pages 139–40 Story of protest in India: Amitav Ghosh, "The Ghosts of Mrs. Gandhi," *The New Yorker*, July 17, 1995.

Page 141 Porter's emerald described in Joan Givner, *Katherine Anne Porter: A Life* (Athens, Ga.: University of Georgia Press, 1991), p. 448.

Page 141 Denis Diderot, *The Indiscreet Jewels*, trans. Sophie Hawkes (New York, N.Y.: Marsilio Publishers, 1993).

Pages 142–43 Blanche Weisen Cook, *Eleanor Roosevelt: Volume 1: 1884–1933* (New York: Penguin, 1993), pp. 230–36.

Page 143 West, op. cit., pp. 16–17.

Pages 143–44 Sojourner Truth, op. cit.

Pages 144–45 On the use of declarations: Tracy Goss, *The Last Word on Power* (New York: Currency/Doubleday, 1995).

Page 145 Wu Yi story: Elsa Walsh, "Profile: Charlene Barshevsky," *The New Yorker*, March 18, 1996.

Page 150 Golda Meir story: Martin, op. cit., p. 304.

Pages 150–51 Melanie Klein story: Grosskurth, op. cit.

Pages 151–52 Mary Lindell story, op. cit.

Page 155 Erna F. Rubinstein, *The Survivor in Us All: Four Young Sisters in the Holocaust* (Hamden, Conn.: Shoestring Press, 1986).

Pages 155–56 Story of Rubinstein's marriage, recounted at the Shoah Foundation training program, Boca Raton, Florida, September 1995.

Page 159 *"wild peace"*: Yehuda Amichai, *Collected Poems* (New York: HarperCollins, 1994).

Page 159 Duncan story: op. cit.

Pages 159–60 Suzanne Farrell story: Shattuck, op. cit.

Page 160 The soldier is James Stockdale. The comment about Epictetus was recounted by Lieutenant Colonel Larry R. Donnithorne, in private conversation.

Pages 161–62 Stockdale's experiences in Vietnam and with Epictetus are recounted in his unpublished paper, "What Is Stoicism?" (August 1993).

SELECT BIBLIOGRAPHY

❦

A Solar Baedeker

Poet Mina Loy wrote a book of poetry and called it *Lunar Baedeker* because it charted her wanderings as an exile and expatriate—a woman on the sidelines of the artistic wars of the early 1900s. The following list of related readings forms a cartography not of the dim sidelines of the imagination but of the forefront of action—the pure daylight world. These books record the habits of those who work by the sun and who would fly to it if they could. Each sheds fantastic light on life, strength, and power. They were my travels, food, and lodging for the three years I devoted to writing this book, and for the previous ten years, which I spent trying to understand power.

Arendt, Hannah, and Karl Jaspers. *Correspondence*. Orlando, Fla.: Harcourt Brace, 1992. Read anything by Hannah Arendt, but especially her letters, for a glimpse of how this brilliant woman learned to live a free life. Jaspers was Arendt's mentor.

Broyard, Anatole. *Intoxicated by My Illness, and Other Writings on Life and Death*. New York: Fawcett, 1992. There is a vast literature of triumph over sickness, but this is the best. Broyard always had a larger than life personality, but when he became ill with prostate cancer, he used the occasion to become more of himself, not less. A sample: "Only by insisting on your style can you keep from falling out of love with yourself as the illness attempts to diminish or disfigure you."

Cather, Willa. *The Song of the Lark*. New York: Signet, 1991. A novel about a girl who grows up on the hardscrabble Midwestern plains to become a singer. "I want only the impossible things," she says. "The others don't interest me."

Cioran, E. M. *Tears and Saints*. Chicago: University of Chicago Press, 1995. The Romanian philosopher's anecdotal history of female mystics.

Coles, Robert. *Simone Weil, A Modern Pilgrimage*. Reading, Mass.: Addison-Wesley, 1989. The life of a modern-day Antigone. Weil died young but influenced poets, statesmen, theologians. As Coles writes, Weil's example focuses the mind and enlarges the heart of all onlookers. Also see Simone Weil's masterpiece, *Gravity and Grace*. New York: Putnam, 1952.

Colette. *Earthly Paradise*. New York: Farrar, Straus & Giroux, 1966. The autobiographical writings of the master of sensuous prose, who says, "Look for a long time at what pleases you, and longer still at what pains you."

David-Neel, Alexandra. *Magic and Mystery in Tibet*. New York: Dover, 1971. The bold travels of a French Orientalist who lived for fourteen years in Tibet, where she experienced spiritual athletics, body heat controls, breathing exercises (when she sent "messages on the wind"), and even the horrors of necromantic magic. Makes all other autobiographical adventures seem like lesser acts.

Dinesen, Isak. *Out of Africa*. New York: Vintage, 1989. Says Dinesen, in these tales of her life as a Kenyan coffee farmer, hunter, cook, lover, woman betrayed, woman victorious, writer of this masterpiece, which she completed in 1936: "A white man who wanted to say a pretty thing to you would write 'I can never forget you.' The African says: 'We do not think of you, that you can ever forget us.' "

Eliot, George. *Daniel Deronda*. London: Oxford University Press, 1984. If any book equals Homer on the wars of state, it is this book on the wars of intimacy. Gwendolyn Harleth is a beautiful young woman "whose confidence lay chiefly in herself," but who comes up against "the strong starch of unexplained rules." Her life and struggles as a "princess in exile."

Haggard, H. Rider. *She*. London: Oxford University Press, 1991. The book that gave birth to the sobriquet "She-who-must-be-obeyed." A fantasy of a warrior princessa with magical powers and undying beauty who takes control of an African tribe.

Harvey, Andrew. *Hidden Journey: A Spiritual Awakening*. New York: Henry Holt, 1991. The story of the author's discovery of Mother Meera, an Indian avatar, and what he learned from her.

Herrera, Hayden. *Frida: A Biography of Frida Kahlo*. New York: Harper & Row, 1983. The life of a painter who, as she described it, "became everything at once in seconds, while my friends became women slowly," when she suffered a near fatal accident. She lived her life at the extremes and reinvented herself many times over.

Ibsen, Henrik. *Hedda Gabler and Other Plays*. New York: Bantam, 1995. Playwrights and novelists have been recasting Medea, the ultimate femme fatale, for centuries. See also Shakespeare's *Macbeth* and Toni Morrison's *Beloved*.

LaBastille, Anne. *Beyond Black Bear Lake*. New York: Norton, 1987. Adventures of a woodswoman who takes Thoreau seriously and builds a cabin in the woods. So mesmerizing you forget you're turning pages.

Pagels, Elaine. *Adam and Eve and the Serpent*. New York: Vintage, 1989. An analysis of the very first words on sex and power.

Rush, Norman. *Mating*. New York: Vintage, 1991. A novel about one of the fiercest female characters in modern fiction. Part comedy, part erotic politics, this is irresistible.

Scarry, Elaine. *The Body in Pain: The Making and Unmaking of the World*. New York: Oxford University Press, 1985. A dense, difficult book that will take you twenty years to read. "Why shouldn't it?" the author once said. "It took me twenty years to write it." It's worth the commitment. An understanding of human vulnerability that is a tour de force.

Steegmuller, Francis, ed. *Flaubert-Sand: The Correspondence*.

New York: Knopf, 1993. Considered by many the finest correspondence of all time. When devastating summer fires nearly destroyed the Berkeley, California, hills several years ago, one report told of a woman who rushed back into her burning home to bring out her copy of this book. In her tragedy, she knew the words of Flaubert and Sand would give her strength. These letters are about their love for each other as a great sustaining bond: George Sand, born Aurore Dupin, was a generation older than Gustave Flaubert and had a son his age.

Watzlawick, Paul. *How Real Is Real? Confusion, Disinformation, Communication.* New York: Vintage, 1977. Goes beyond Deborah Tannen to the guts of communications strategy—all to make reality more real, not less.

Poet-Fighters

The truest glimpses of the wars of intimacy always come from poets. They wrap their soft fists in iron gloves.

Akhmatova, Anna. *Poems.* New York: Norton, 1983.

Bishop, Elizabeth. *The Complete Poems, 1927–1979.* New York: Noonday, 1993.

The Book of Psalms. King David's songs describe a subservience to powers larger than the ones this conqueror/poet claimed for himself. David's name means "lover"; no wonder the Old Testament's greatest conqueror combines intricate knowledge of creation and destruction.

Graham, Jorie. *The End of Beauty.* Hopewell, N.J.: Ecco Press, 1987.

Kinsella, Thomas, trans. *The Tain.* London: Oxford University

Press, 1969. The eighth-century Irish epic. A husband and wife, king and queen, stage an epic battle in which women warriors play important roles.

Tagore, Rabindranath. *Collected Poems and Plays*. New York: Collier Books/Macmillan, 1993. Tagore's play *Chitra* is about "the power of the weak and the weapon of the unarmed hand."

Tsvetayeva, Marina. *After Russia*. Ann Arbor, Mich.: Ardis, 1992.

Classics on Power

Besides Machiavelli's *The Prince* and Sun Tzu's *The Art of War*, there are three books that describe the foundations of the power that built the world:

De Jouvenel, Bertrand. *On Power: The Natural History of Its Growth*. Indianapolis, Ind.: Liberty Fund, 1993. The 1945 bible on command-and-control methodologies.

Foucault, Michel. *Power/Knowledge*. New York: Pantheon, 1980. Brilliant essays on, among other things, truth and power, sight and power, sex and power.

Russell, Bertrand. *Power*. New York: Routledge, 1993. What Freud did for sex, Russell does for power. The forms, limits, curlicues of human nature in the grip of the big ambition. Unfortunately, he never analyzes the power his lover, Ottoline Morrell, held over him.

ACKNOWLEDGMENTS

Twenty years in this business of publishing led me to think I knew everything there was to know about creating a book. But if I hadn't had the luck to meet up with three geniuses, this book could never have been written. I thank them in the order in which they came into my life.

Betty Sue Flowers, professor of English at the University of Texas at Austin, is a knower. You don't have to raise a question with her—she shows up at the right moment with the answers. The word "brilliance" belongs to her. Betty Sue taught me how to go beyond reading poetry into seeing poetry in everything. She is a holdover from the days when Homer wasn't too blind to look into the sky, see beautiful blond geniuses, and call them goddesses.

Sandra Dijkstra I'd known for years as a literary agent before I ever dreamed she would be *my* agent. As much as I fear her in my role as editor—there is no tougher agent—I cherish her as an author. She read draft after draft, coached, encouraged, inspired, offered the depth of her own insight from her own marvelous book, *Flora Tristan*. She is a rare combination—creativity devoted to the service of her authors.

Of Betsy Lerner I stand in awe, and such "of thee I sing" locutions are apt. Betsy is a nation state in the form of a person. She is a genius in her own right, full of stunning ideas about people, processes, and things. As my editor, she humbled me; I thought I knew my profession and business, but she taught me so much. Through draft after draft, Betsy stayed firm to a vision about books, a ferocious standard of quality. Anyone who comes into Betsy's life is lucky beyond compare.

Many people at Doubleday gave their time, energy, and creativity. I began to feel like the Sultana of Brunei when I would arrive at my desk day after day to find riches waiting for me in the form of encouragement, suggestions, artwork, cover copy. Mario Pulice gave *The Princessa* its beautiful cover, as he has given me so many wonderful covers for Currency books in the past. My closest Currency colleagues, Jennifer Breheny, Lisa Brancaccio, Michael Iannazzi, and Laurel Cook, were always ready with life-sustaining suggestions and encouragement. Each of them is a force of genius in his or her own right. Arlene Friedman, Doubleday's publisher, has been a godsend of a boss, giving me the support to finish this book and being a wise judge over the publishing process. Michael Palgon is a firm, guiding hand in the most difficult parts of the business. Pat Mulcahy, Doubleday's editor in chief, has taught me a thing or two about grace and laughter. Brandon Saltz and Laura Hodes, Doubleday assistants, take on the difficult work of author intervention with uncommon poise. Nan Talese's conversation has been a drink of cool water to me in the times I felt like a desert traveler in this business. Kathy Trager, Paula Breen, Carol Lazare, Janet Hill, and, of course, Emma Bolton are model princessas whom I watched and learned from. Tom Cahill has made it almost impossible to take on the double job of editing and writing, because he is a superior example of both breeds; it's been a joy to see him do brilliantly at both skills.

I owe Stephen Rubin, now president of Doubleday's international division, a great debt. He was one of the prime movers of this project, as was David Gernert, of Gernert Industries. Bill Barry, now Doubleday's head of Operations, has been an unfailing source of inspiration, insight, and scruples. These three magi hardly need a book about power, but they made it possible for this one to exist. Martha Levin, publisher of Anchor Books, has re-created a venerable publishing program into a list more distinguished than ever, so it was no surprise to me when, at an editorial meeting three years ago, she turned to me and said, "You should write a book about power." She is always creating books, even in the most unlikely places.

This is an allegorical world, so of course Jack Hoeft, Doubleday's CEO, not only should look like a legendary elm tree but should also fit the adjective "towering" in many inspiring ways. "Beloved" isn't a word that fits most corporate leaders; but it certainly fits Jack, whom people admire and enjoy. I've never known Jack to be anything but Machiavella-ian. It has been a privilege to be his employee and now one of his authors.

And of my authors, I can say no editor has been blessed with better. They have been my teachers for the almost ten years of Currency's existence. I have learned from the best, but particularly from Andy Grove, CEO and chairman of the board of Intel, who taught me that paranoia was good; but he is nothing if not the target of pronoia. Dee Hock, founder and chairman emeritus of Visa, taught me that command-and-control power is over, and that women have much more power than men. Peter Senge of MIT is a teacher of such light and spirit that you'd think you were working and studying in Paradise. Jack Stack of Springfield Remanufacturing taught me to see beauty and freedom in the everyday. Bo Burlingham, *Inc.* magazine editor at large, has a voice of humanity that is so generous I couldn't help trying to model my own after it. Jacob Needleman, philosopher, pure soul: you can't be in Jerry's presence for more than a minute without thinking, How did the universe get so lucky to have a translator like him to make sense of it? Christopher Maurer of Vanderbilt University, Art Kleiner, and David Whyte have given Currency brilliant books that changed my thinking. Barry Nalebuff and Adam Brandenburger opened my eyes to the possibilities of an overall change-the-game strategy, which they use as the basis of game theory in their marvelous book, *Co-opetition.* Tracy Goss's book *The Last Word on Power* and her course on executive reinvention changed my life, and countless others' lives besides. Sally Helgesen is a figure of great authority in women's leadership, and her book, *The Female Advantage*, has been important to me. Roseanne by her very existence is a teacher of the first order; she is smart, wise, and a fierce woman warrior. Werner Erhard is first among men, thinkers, and exhilarating conversationalists. Napier Collyns has been an intellectual banquet for the ten years I've known him. Roger Ailes and Jon Kraushar are two powers in their own right; just to be near them is to begin to understand how it's possible to be so gifted and such mensches at the same time.

I have also been enriched by knowing those two wise young owls Alan Webber and Bill Taylor, cocreators of the marvelous new magazine *Fast Company*. Herbert Allen, of Allen and Company, gave me a serious education not only in power but, more important, in the power of forgiveness. Mickey Schulhof and Paola Schulhof are masters of the ease and generosity of power. George Gendron, editor in chief of *Inc.*, thinks fascinating thoughts before anyone else in the world begins to catch on. Deb Futter of Random House read early drafts and was kind enough to say, Keep going. Great thanks go to Rita Holm of the Sandra Dijkstra Agency, who offered her critiques with the life-saving insight and delicacy that a brain surgeon could learn from. Bob Daniels, Doubleday copy editor, deserves praise for being, as Henry James once put it, "finely aware and richly responsible." His comments on the manuscript were as painstaking and beautifying as Flemish embroidery. I am in his debt.

I felt like a beggar at a banquet's seat of honor twice a month in the fall of 1994 and the winter of 1995, when I was named a guest fellow at Brown University's Pembroke Research Seminar on "The Question of Violence." Ellen Rooney directed a group of amazing scholars who met to study their papers and others', from Thomas De Quincy to Slavoj Zizek.

My family has been the basis of much encouragement. My brother, Harold Rubin, is a leader and power in his own right, president of Midland Memorial Hospital in Midland, Texas. What older brother isn't always the key to a woman's views about power? My mother, Sadie Rubin, pushed and prodded me into the habit of independence. She is herself a warrior par excellence. The late Bernard Rubin, my father, tried to build a world in which power and love were distinctions without a difference. Yugo, Otto, and Honeybear are three beautiful memories that will always be with me; so, too, are my memories of Bob Marcinczyk.

Marty Leaf I would wish on every woman with an idea, a dream, and a colossal problem. Marty is a high-powered New York lawyer (at Morrison Cohen Singer and Weinstein), an intellectual, and a full-time savior. I once read a book that described Moses as a "motherly father," and that description fits Marty, who knows the law and practices it with the most elegant, gentle sympathy.

Lastly, Avram Miller, brilliant technologist, leader, metaphysician, to whom this book is dedicated. He taught me love and war and if that wasn't enough the most valuable lesson any princessa can learn: that it's foolish to try to imagine the future when you can just create it.